# DOVER · THRIFT · EDITIONS

# Love's Labour's Lost

# WILLIAM SHAKESPEARE

## DOVER PUBLICATIONS, INC.
### Mineola, New York

GENERAL EDITOR: PAUL NEGRI
EDITOR OF THIS VOLUME: SUSAN L. RATTINER

*Copyright*

*Theatrical Rights*

This Dover Thrift Edition may be used in its entirety, in adaptation, or in any other way for theatrical productions, professional and amateur, in the United States, without fee, permission, or acknowledgment. (This may not apply outside of the United States, as copyright conditions may vary.)

*Bibliographical Note*

This Dover edition, first published in 2001, contains the unabridged text of *Love's Labour's Lost* as published in Volume II of *The Caxton Edition of the Complete Works of William Shakespeare*, Caxton Publishing Company, London, n.d. The Note was prepared specially for this edition.

*Library of Congress Cataloging-in-Publication Data*

Shakespeare, William, 1564–1616.
    Love's labour's lost / William Shakespeare.
        p. cm. — (Dover thrift editions)
    ISBN 0-486-41929-0 (pbk.)
    1. Navarre (Kingdom)—Drama. 2. Courts and courtiers—Drama. 3. Princesses—Drama. I. Title. II. Series.

PR2822.A1 2001
822.3'3—dc21

2001047272

Manufactured in the United States by Courier Corporation
41929002
www.doverpublications.com

# Note

WILLIAM SHAKESPEARE (1564–1616) was born in Stratford-on-Avon, Warwickshire, England. Although much of his early life remains sketchy, it is known that he moved to London ca. 1589 to earn his way as an actor and playwright. He joined an acting company known as the Lord Chamberlain's Mēn in 1594, a decision that finally enabled him to share in the financial success of his plays. Only eighteen of his thirty-seven plays were published during his lifetime, and these were usually sold directly to theater companies and printed in quartos, or single-play editions, without his approval.

*Love's Labour's Lost*, first performed in 1594, is regarded as one of Shakespeare's earliest works in the canon of his thirty-seven plays. Bearing in mind that there is no entry found for the play in the Stationers' *Register*, critics and scholars suspect that the first edition of the work was a bad quarto edition that was lost, and has since been superseded by the First Quarto of 1598. It is generally acknowledged among Shakespearean scholars that *Love's Labour's Lost* is probably Shakespeare's first comedy, and as such, is often treated as an experimental piece in his development as a dramatist.

In contrast to many of Shakespeare's works, *Love's Labour's Lost* appears to be an original composition, the first one he wrote that has no known source for the plot. Most of his works are a credit to his ability to meld a variety of different sources into a pastiche of sorts, resulting in his own creation of a play. In some cases, however, Shakespeare wrote plays for special social events such as weddings or court occasions. An example of this is *The Merry Wives of Windsor*, which was written and performed at the specific request of Queen Elizabeth. Whether the derivation of his work stemmed from traditional medieval legend, classic literature, contemporary chronicles, or dramas of the day, Shakespeare nonetheless excelled at portraying the foibles of the human condition.

# Contents

# Contents

# Dramatis Personæ[1]

FERDINAND, king of Navarre.

BIRON,
LONGAVILLE, } lords attending on the King.
DUMAIN,

BOYET,
MERCADE, } lords attending on the Princess of France.

DON ADRIANO DE ARMADO, a fantastical Spaniard.

SIR NATHANIEL, a curate.

HOLOFERNES, a schoolmaster.

DULL, a constable.

COSTARD, a clown.

MOTH, page to Armado.

A Forester.

The PRINCESS of France.

ROSALINE,
MARIA, } ladies attending on the Princess.
KATHARINE,

JAQUENETTA, a country wench.

Lords, Attendants, &c.
SCENE—*Navarre*

[1]This play was first printed in quarto in 1598. The quarto edition was reprinted with tri-
fling changes in the First Folio of 1623. A second quarto edition of 1631 reprints the
First Folio version. No list of *dramatis personæ* is given in any of the early editions. This
was first supplied by Rowe in his edition of Shakespeare's works, 1709. The first quarto
does not divide the play into either acts or scenes. The First Folio divides it into acts
alone. Rowe first subdivided the acts into scenes.

# ACT I.

## SCENE I. *Navarre. A Park, Near a Palace.*

*Enter the* KING, BIRON, LONGAVILLE, *and* DUMAIN

KING.    Let fame, that all hunt after in their lives,
    Live register'd upon our brazen tombs,
    And then grace us in the disgrace of death;
    When, spite of cormorant devouring Time,
    The endeavour of this present breath may buy
    That honour which shall bate his scythe's keen edge,
    And make us heirs of all eternity.
    Therefore, brave conquerors,—for so you are,
    That war against your own affections
    And the huge army of the world's desires,—    10
    Our late edict shall strongly stand in force:
    Navarre shall be the wonder of the world;
    Our court shall be a little Academe,
    Still and contemplative in living art.
    You three, Biron, Dumain, and Longaville,
    Have sworn for three years' term to live with me
    My fellow-scholars, and to keep those statutes
    That are recorded in this schedule here:
    Your oaths are pass'd; and now subscribe your names,
    That his own hand may strike his honour down    20
    That violates the smallest branch herein:
    If you are arm'd to do as sworn to do,
    Subscribe to your deep oaths, and keep it too.
LONG.    I am resolved; 't is but a three years' fast:
    The mind shall banquet, though the body pine:
    Fat paunches have lean pates; and dainty bits
    Make rich the ribs, but bankrupt quite the wits.
DUM.    My loving lord, Dumain is mortified:
    The grosser manner of these world's delights

1

He throws upon the gross world's baser slaves:                    30
To love, to wealth, to pomp, I pine and die;
With all these living in philosophy.

BIRON.   I can but say their protestation over;
So much, dear liege, I have already sworn,
That is, to live and study here three years.
But there are other strict observances;
As, not to see a woman in that term,
Which I hope well is not enrolled there;
And one day in a week to touch no food,
And but one meal on every day beside,                             40
The which I hope is not enrolled there;
And then, to sleep but three hours in the night,
And not be seen to wink of all the day,—
When I was wont to think no harm all night,
And make a dark night too of half the day,—
Which I hope well is not enrolled there:
O, these are barren tasks, too hard to keep,
Not to see ladies, study, fast, not sleep!

KING.   Your oath is pass'd to pass away from these.

BIRON.   Let me say no, my liege, an if you please:               50
I only swore to study with your grace,
And stay here in your court for three years' space.

LONG.   You swore to that, Biron, and to the rest.

BIRON.   By yea and nay, sir, then I swore in jest.
What is the end of study? let me know.

KING.   Why, that to know, which else we should not know.

BIRON.   Things hid and barr'd, you mean, from common sense?

KING.   Ay, that is study's god-like recompence.

BIRON.   Come on, then; I will swear to study so,
To know the thing I am forbid to know:                            60
As thus,—to study where I well may dine,
    When I to feast expressly am forbid;
Or study where to meet some mistress fine,
    When mistresses from common sense are hid;
Or, having sworn too hard a keeping oath,
Study to break it, and not break my troth.
If study's gain be thus, and this be so,
Study knows that which yet it doth not know:
Swear me to this, and I will ne'er say no.

---

43 *of all the day*] all the day long.
57 *common sense*] the light of nature; cf. line 75, "the light of truth."
62 *feast*] Theobald's obviously correct emendation of the *fast* of the earlier editions.

KING.     These be the stops that hinder study quite,                    70
    And train our intellects to vain delight.
BIRON.   Why, all delights are vain; but that most vain,
    Which, with pain purchased, doth inherit pain:
    As, painfully to pore upon a book
        To seek the light of truth; while truth the while
    Doth falsely blind the eyesight of his look:
        Light, seeking light, doth light of light beguile:
    So, ere you find where light in darkness lies,
    Your light grows dark by losing of your eyes.
    Study me how to please the eye indeed,                    80
        By fixing it upon a fairer eye;
    Who dazzling so, that eye shall be his heed,
        And give him light that it was blinded by.
    Study is like the heaven's glorious sun,
        That will not be deep search'd with saucy looks:
    Small have continual plodders ever won,
        Save base authority from others' books.
    These earthly godfathers of heaven's lights,
        That give a name to every fixed star,
    Have no more profit of their shining nights                    90
        Than those that walk and wot not what they are.
    Too much to know, is to know nought but fame;
    And every godfather can give a name.
KING.     How well he's read, to reason against reading!
DUM.     Proceeded well, to stop all good proceeding!
LONG.    He weeds the corn, and still lets grow the weeding.
BIRON.   The spring is near, when green geese are a-breeding.
DUM.     How follows that?
BIRON.                      Fit in his place and time.
DUM.     In reason nothing.                                            100
BIRON.                     Something, then, in rhyme.
KING.     Biron is like an envious sneaping frost,
        That bites the first-born infants of the spring.
BIRON.   Well, say I am; why should proud summer boast,
        Before the birds have any cause to sing?
    Why should I joy in any abortive birth?
    At Christmas I no more desire a rose

77–79 *Light, seeking . . . your eyes*] The sense is, that a man by too close study may read
    himself blind.
80–83 *Study me . . . blinded by*] When the eye has been dazzled or half-blinded by fix-
    ing its gaze on a "fairer eye," that "fairer eye" shall become its "heed," or lode-star,
    and give back to it the light of which it has been deprived.
95 *Proceeded*] A quibble upon the academic use of this word for graduating.

Than wish a snow in May's new-fangled shows;
But like of each thing that in season grows.
So you, to study now it is too late,                                    110
Climb o'er the house to unlock the little gate.
KING.   Well, sit you out: go home, Biron: adieu.
BIRON.   No, my good lord; I have sworn to stay with you:
And though I have for barbarism spoke more
    Than for that angel knowledge you can say,
Yet confident I'll keep what I have swore,
    And bide the penance of each three years' day
Give me the paper; let me read the same;
And to the strict'st decrees I'll write my name.
KING.   How well this yielding rescues thee from shame!     120
BIRON.   [*reads*]   "Item, That no woman shall come within a mile of
my court,"—Hath this been proclaimed?
LONG.   Four days ago.
BIRON.   Let's see the penalty. [*Reads*] "on pain of losing her
tongue." Who devised this penalty?
LONG.   Marry, that did I.
BIRON.   Sweet lord, and why?
LONG.   To fright them hence with that dread penalty.
BIRON.   A dangerous law against gentility!
[*Reads*] "Item, If any man be seen to talk with a woman within the term     130
of three years, he shall endure such public shame as the rest of the
court can possibly devise."
This article, my liege, yourself must break;
    For well you know here comes in embassy
The French king's daughter with yourself to speak,—
    A maid of grace and complete majesty,—
About surrender up of Aquitaine
    To her decrepit, sick, and bedrid father:
Therefore this article is made in vain,
    Or vainly comes the admired princess hither.     140
KING.   What say you, lords? why, this was quite forgot.
BIRON.   So study evermore is overshot:
While it doth study to have what it would,
It doth forget to do the thing it should;
And when it hath the thing it hunteth most,
'T is won as towns with fire, so won, so lost.
KING.   We must of force dispense with this decree;
She must lie here on mere necessity.

112 *sit you out*] stand out, take no part; an expression used in connection with indoor
   games.

BIRON.    Necessity will make us all forsworn
       Three thousand times within this three years' space;      150
   For every man with his affects is born,
       Not by might master'd, but by special grace:
   If I break faith, this word shall speak for me,
   I am forsworn on "mere necessity."
   So to the laws at large I write my name:        [*Subscribes.*
       And he that breaks them in the least degree
   Stands in attainder of eternal shame:
       Suggestions are to other as to me;
   But I believe, although I seem so loth,
   I am the last that will last keep his oath.      160
   But is there no quick recreation granted?
KING.    Ay, that there is. Our court, you know, is haunted
       With a refined traveller of Spain;
   A man in all the world's new fashion planted,
       That hath a mint of phrases in his brain;
   One whom the music of his own vain tongue
       Doth ravish like enchanting harmony;
   A man of complements, whom right and wrong
       Have chose as umpire of their mutiny:
   This child of fancy, that Armado hight,      170
       For interim to our studies, shall relate,
   In high-born words, the worth of many a knight
       From tawny Spain, lost in the world's debate.
   How you delight, my lords, I know not, I;
   But, I protest, I love to hear him lie,
   And I will use him for my minstrelsy.
BIRON.    Armado is a most illustrious wight,
   A man of fire-new words, fashion's own knight.
LONG.    Costard the swain and he shall be our sport;
   And, so to study, three years is but short.      180

*Enter* DULL *with a letter, and* COSTARD

DULL.    Which is the Duke's own person?
BIRON.    This, fellow: what wouldst?
DULL.    I myself reprehend his own person, for I am his Grace's

---

149–160 *Necessity . . . his oath*] These twelve lines are formed of two sixains, or six-line stanzas, rhyming *ababcc* (cf. IV, iii, 219–224, *infra*). This is the metre of Shakespeare's *Venus and Adonis*, and of much narrative verse of the period. It is rarely used in drama.

tharborough: but I would see his own person in flesh and
blood.

BIRON.　This is he.

DULL.　Signior Arme—Arme—commends you. There's villany
abroad: this letter will tell you more.

COST.　Sir, the contempts thereof are as touching me.

KING.　A letter from the magnificent Armado.　　　　　　　　190

BIRON.　How low soever the matter, I hope in God for high
words.

LONG.　A high hope for a low heaven: God grant us patience!

BIRON.　To hear? or forbear laughing?

LONG.　To hear meekly, sir, and to laugh moderately; or to forbear both.

BIRON.　Well, sir, be it as the style shall give us cause to climb in
the merriness.

COST.　The matter is to me, sir, as concerning Jaquenetta. The
matter of it is, I was taken with the manner.　　　　　　200

BIRON.　In what manner?

COST.　In manner and form following, sir; all those three: I was
seen with her in the manor-house, sitting with her upon the
form, and taken following her into the park; which, put together, is in manner and form following. Now, sir, for the
manner,—it is the manner of a man to speak to a woman:
for the form,—in some form.

BIRON.　For the following, sir?

COST.　As it shall follow in my correction: and God defend the
right!　　　　　　　　　　　　　　　　　　　　　　　　210

KING.　Will you hear this letter with attention?

BIRON.　As we would hear an oracle.

COST.　Such is the simplicity of man to hearken after the flesh.

KING.　[*reads*] "Great deputy, the welkin's vicegerent, and sole
dominator of Navarre, my soul's earth's god, and body's fostering
patron."—

COST.　Not a word of Costard yet.

KING.　[*reads*]　"So it is,"—

COST.　It may be so: but if he says it is so, he is, in telling true,
but so.　　　　　　　　　　　　　　　　　　　　　　　220

---

184 *tharborough*] third-borough, constable. Thus the First Folio. The first quarto reads
*Farborough*, doubtless by way of reproducing the constable's mispronunciation.

200 *taken with the manner*] "in flagrante delicto." According to Cowell's Law Dictionary
(1607), "Mainour alias manour . . . in a legal sense denoteth the thing that a thief
taketh or stealeth; as to be *taken with the mainour* is to be taken with the thing
stolen about him."

KING.  Peace!

COST.  Be to me, and every man that dares not fight!

KING.  No words!

COST.  Of other men's secrets, I beseech you.

KING.  [*reads*]  "So it is, besieged with sable-coloured melancholy, I
did commend the black-oppressing humour to the most whole-
some physic of thy health-giving air; and, as I am a gentleman, be-
took myself to walk. The time when? About the sixth hour; when
beasts most graze, birds best peck, and men sit down to that nour-
ishment which is called supper: so much for the time when. Now      230
for the ground which; which, I mean, I walked upon: it is ycleped
thy park. Then for the place where; where, I mean, I did encounter
that obscene and most preposterous event, that draweth from my
snow-white pen the ebon-coloured ink, which here thou viewest,
beholdest, surveyest, or seest: but to the place where, — it standeth
north-north-east and by east from the west corner of thy curious-
knotted garden: there did I see that low-spirited swain, that base
minnow of thy mirth," —

COST.  Me?

KING.  [*reads*]  "that unlettered small-knowing soul," —                 240

COST.  Me?

KING.  [*reads*]  "that shallow vassal," —

COST.  Still me?

KING.  [*reads*]  "which, as I remember, hight Costard," —

COST.  O, me!

KING.  [*reads*]  "sorted and consorted, contrary to thy established proclaimed edict and continent canon, which with, — O, with — but
with this I passion to say wherewith," —

COST.  With a wench.

KING.  [*reads*]  "with a child of our grandmother Eve, a female; or, for      250
thy more sweet understanding, a woman. Him I, as my ever-
esteemed duty pricks me on, have sent to thee, to receive the meed
of punishment, by thy sweet Grace's officer, Anthony Dull; a man
of good repute, carriage, bearing, and estimation."

DULL.  Me, an 't shall please you: I am Anthony Dull.

KING.  [*reads*]  "For Jaquenetta, — so is the weaker vessel called which
I apprehended with the aforesaid swain, — I keep her as a vessel of
thy law's fury; and shall, at the least of thy sweet notice, bring her
to trial. Thine, in all compliment of devoted and heart-burning
heat of duty.                    DON ADRIANO DE ARMADO."      260

---

236–237 *curious-knotted*]  with flower-beds intersecting one another with some compli-
cation.

256, 257 *vessel*]  The word is used as in the New Testament; both the lines in which it
figures echo scriptural phrases.

BIRON.   This is not so well as I looked for, but the best that ever
        I heard.
KING.   Ay, the best for the worst. But, sirrah, what say you to this?
COST.   Sir, I confess the wench.
KING.   Did you hear the proclamation?
COST.   I do confess much of the hearing it, but little of the mark-
        ing of it.
KING.   It was proclaimed a year's imprisonment, to be taken
        with a wench.
COST.   I was taken with none, sir: I was taken with a damsel.     270
KING.   Well, it was proclaimed damsel.
COST.   This was no damsel neither, sir; she was a virgin.
KING.   It is so varied too; for it was proclaimed virgin.
COST.   If it were, I deny her virginity; I was taken with a maid.
KING.   This maid will not serve your turn, sir.
COST.   This maid will serve my turn, sir.
KING.   Sir, I will pronounce your sentence: you shall fast a week
        with bran and water.
COST.   I had rather pray a month with mutton and porridge.
KING.   And Don Armado shall be your keeper.     280
        My Lord Biron, see him deliver'd o'er:
        And go we, lords, to put in practice that
        Which each to other hath so strongly sworn.

                    [*Exeunt* KING, LONGAVILLE, *and* DUMAIN.

BIRON.   I'll lay my head to any good man's hat,
        These oaths and laws will prove an idle scorn.
        Sirrah, come on.
COST.   I suffer for the truth, sir; for true it is, I was taken with
        Jaquenetta, and Jaquenetta is a true girl; and, therefore, wel-
        come the sour cup of prosperity! Affliction may one day
        smile again; and till then, sit thee down, sorrow!     290

                                        [*Exeunt*.

## SCENE II. *The Same.*

*Enter* ARMADO *and* MOTH *his Page*

ARM.   Boy, what sign is it when a man of great spirit grows
        melancholy?
MOTH.   A great sign, sir, that he will look sad.
ARM.   Why, sadness is one and the self-same thing, dear imp.
MOTH.   No, no; O Lord, sir, no.

ARM.  How canst thou part sadness and melancholy, my tender
 juvenal?
MOTH.  By a familiar demonstration of the working, my tough
 senior.
ARM.  Why tough senior? why tough senior?                          10
MOTH.  Why tender juvenal? why tender juvenal?
ARM.  I spoke it, tender juvenal, as a congruent epitheton
 appertaining to thy young days, which we may nominate
 tender.
MOTH.  And I, tough senior, as an appertinent title to your old
 time, which we may name tough.
ARM.  Pretty and apt.
MOTH.  How mean you, sir? I pretty, and my saying apt? or I apt,
 and my saying pretty?
ARM.  Thou pretty, because little.                                 20
MOTH.  Little pretty, because little. Wherefore apt?
ARM.  And therefore apt, because quick.
MOTH.  Speak you this in my praise, master?
ARM.  In thy condign praise.
MOTH.  I will praise an eel with the same praise.
ARM.  What, that an eel is ingenious?
MOTH.  That an eel is quick.
ARM.  I do say thou art quick in answers: thou heatest my blood.
MOTH.  I am answered, sir.
ARM.  I love not to be crossed.                                    30
MOTH. [Aside]  He speaks the mere contrary; crosses love not
 him.
ARM.  I have promised to study three years with the Duke.
MOTH.  You may do it in an hour, sir.
ARM.  Impossible.
MOTH.  How many is one thrice told?
ARM.  I am ill at reckoning; it fitteth the spirit of a tapster.
MOTH.  You are a gentleman and a gamester, sir.
ARM.  I confess both: they are both the varnish of a complete
 man.                                                              40
MOTH.  Then, I am sure, you know how much the gross sum of
 deuce-ace amounts to.
ARM.  It doth amount to one more than two.
MOTH.  Which the base vulgar do call three.
ARM.  True.

---

31 crosses] The pun here turns on the use of the word in the sense of money, i.e. coins
 stamped with a cross.

MOTH. Why, sir, is this such a piece of study? Now here is three studied, ere ye'll thrice wink: and how easy it is to put years to the word three, and study three years in two words, the dancing horse will tell you.

ARM. A most fine figure! 50

MOTH. To prove you a cipher.

ARM. I will hereupon confess I am in love: and as it is base for a soldier to love, so am I in love with a base wench. If drawing my sword against the humour of affection would deliver me from the reprobate thought of it, I would take Desire prisoner, and ransom him to any French courtier for a new-devised courtesy. I think scorn to sigh: methinks I should outswear Cupid. Comfort me, boy: what great men have been in love?

MOTH. Hercules, master. 60

ARM. Most sweet Hercules! More authority, dear boy, name more; and, sweet my child, let them be men of good repute and carriage.

MOTH. Samson, master: he was a man of good carriage, great carriage, for he carried the town-gates on his back like a porter: and he was in love.

ARM. O well-knit Samson! strong-jointed Samson! I do excel thee in my rapier as much as thou didst me in carrying gates. I am in love too. Who was Samson's love, my dear Moth?

MOTH. A woman, master. 70

ARM. Of what complexion?

MOTH. Of all the four, or the three, or the two, or one of the four.

ARM. Tell me precisely of what complexion.

MOTH. Of the sea-water green, sir.

ARM. Is that one of the four complexions?

MOTH. As I have read, sir; and the best of them too.

49 *the dancing horse*] A reference to a clever performing horse known as *Marocco* or *Morocco*, which was for many years towards the end of the sixteenth century exhibited in London and the chief cities of England and the continent by its master, a Staffordshire man, named Bankes. Numerous references to the animal's powers of dancing and of solving arithmetical puzzles, to which allusion is made in the text, figure in contemporary literature.

71 *complexion*] Used in the double sense of "colour of the face" and "humour" or "temperament" of the body. The humours or temperaments were held in contemporary medicine to be *four* in number, *viz.*: the phlegmatic, choleric, sanguine, and melancholy, and all were credited with distinguishing hues. No complexion (in the sense of "humour") was, of course, of a "sea-water green" colour. But an ordinary symptom of chlorosis, or the "green sickness," from which young growing girls suffered, was a pale, greenish complexion.

ARM.   Green, indeed, is the colour of lovers; but to have a love
       of that color, methinks Samson had small reason for it. He
       surely affected her for her wit.                                80
MOTH.  It was so, sir; for she had a green wit.
ARM.   My love is most immaculate white and red.
MOTH.  Most maculate thoughts, master, are masked under
       such colours.
ARM.   Define, define, well-educated infant.
MOTH.  My father's wit, and my mother's tongue, assist me!
ARM.   Sweet invocation of a child; most pretty and pathetical!
MOTH.  If she be made of white and red,
           Her faults will ne'er be known;
       For blushing cheeks by faults are bred,                         90
           And fears by pale white shown:
       Then if she fear, or be to blame,
           By this you shall not know;
       For still her cheeks possess the same
           Which native she doth owe.
       A dangerous rhyme, master, against the reason of white and
       red.
ARM.   Is there not a ballad, boy, of the King and the Beggar?
MOTH.  The world was very guilty of such a ballad some three
       ages since: but, I think, now 't is not to be found; or, if it    100
       were, it would neither serve for the writing nor the tune.
ARM.   I will have that subject newly writ o'er, that I may exam-
       ple my digression by some mighty precedent. Boy, I do love
       that country girl that I took in the park with the rational hind
       Costard: she deserves well.
MOTH. [Aside]  To be whipped; and yet a better love than my
       master.
ARM.   Sing, boy; my spirit grows heavy in love.
MOTH.  And that's great marvel, loving a light wench.
ARM.   I say, sing.                                                     110
MOTH.  Forbear till this company be past.

Enter DULL, COSTARD, and JAQUENETTA

DULL.  Sir, the duke's pleasure is, that you keep Costard safe:

81 green wit] There may be a punning reference here to the green withes wherewith
   Delilah bound Samson.
98 King . . . Beggar] The ballad of King Cophetua's courtship of the beggar-maid fig-
   ured in Richard Johnson's The Crown-Garland, 1612, under the title of "A Song of a
   Beggar and a King." The piece is included in Percy's Reliques (1877), I, 189–194.
   Shakespeare refers to the story again (infra, IV, i, 66–67 seq.); and in Rom. and Jul.,
   II, i, 14. King Cophetua is mentioned in 2 Hen. IV, V, iii, 106.

and you must suffer him to take no delight nor no penance;
but a' must fast three days a week. For this damsel, I must
keep her at the park: she is allowed for the day-woman. Fare
you well.

ARM.   I do betray myself with blushing. Maid.

JAQ.   Man.

ARM.   I will visit thee at the lodge.

JAQ.   That's hereby.                                              120

ARM.   I know where it is situate.

JAQ.   Lord, how wise you are!

ARM.   I will tell thee wonders.

JAQ.   With that face?

ARM.   I love thee.

JAQ.   So I heard you say.

ARM.   And so, farewell.

JAQ.   Fair weather after you!

DULL.   Come, Jaquenetta, away!

                              [*Exeunt* DULL *and* JAQUENETTA.

ARM.   Villain, thou shalt fast for thy offences ere thou be     130
pardoned.

COST.   Well, sir, I hope, when I do it, I shall do it on a full
stomach.

ARM.   Thou shalt be heavily punished.

COST.   I am more bound to you than your fellows, for they are
but lightly rewarded.

ARM.   Take away this villain; shut him up.

MOTH.   Come, you transgressing slave; away!

COST.   Let me not be pent up, sir: I will fast, being loose.

MOTH.   No, sir; that were fast and loose: thou shalt to prison.  140

COST.   Well, if ever I do see the merry days of desolation that I
have seen, some shall see.

MOTH.   What shall some see?

COST.   Nay, nothing, Master Moth, but what they look upon. It
is not for prisoners to be too silent in their words; and therefore I will say nothing: I thank God I have as little patience
as another man; and therefore I can be quiet.

                              [*Exeunt* MOTH *and* COSTARD.

---

140 *fast and loose*] A cheating game much practised by gipsies, and sometimes called
"pricking at the belt." Separate strips of leather were so arranged on a table as to present the appearance of a belt in a single piece. The player was invited to thrust a
skewer into the leather so as to attach it to the table on which it was placed, and
bets were laid whether he would make the pretended belt fast or loose.

ARM.    I do affect the very ground, which is base, where her shoe,
     which is baser, guided by her foot, which is basest, doth
     tread. I shall be forsworn, which is a great argument of false-     150
     hood, if I love. And how can that be true love which is falsely
     attempted? Love is a familiar; Love is a devil: there is no evil
     angel but Love. Yet was Samson so tempted, and he had an
     excellent strength; yet was Soloman so seduced, and he had
     a very good wit. Cupid's butt-shaft is too hard for Hercules'
     club; and therefore too much odds for a Spaniard's rapier.
     The first and second cause will not serve my turn; the pas-
     sado he respects not, the duello he regards not: his disgrace
     is to be called boy; but his glory is to subdue men. Adieu, val-
     our! rust, rapier! be still, drum! for your manager is in love;     160
     yea, he loveth. Assist me some extemporal god of rhyme, for
     I am sure I shall turn sonnet. Devise, wit; write, pen; for I am
     for whole volumes in folio.                                [*Exit.*

157 *first and second cause*] "Cause" was often used in the technical sense of ground for
    a challenge to a duel. The various "causes" which were formally recognized by du-
    ellists are described in *"Vincentio Saviolo His Practise, in two Bookes. The first in-
    treating of the use of the Rapier and Dagger. The second, of honor and honorable
    quarrels."* 1595.

# ACT II.

## SCENE I. *The Same.*

*Enter the* PRINCESS OF FRANCE, ROSALINE, MARIA, KATHARINE,
    BOYET, Lords, *and other* Attendants

BOYET.   Now, Madam, Summon up your dearest spirits:
    Consider who the king your father sends;
    To whom he sends; and what's his embassy:
    Yourself, held precious in the world's esteem,
    To parley with the sole inheritor
    Of all perfections that a man may owe,
    Matchless Navarre; the plea of no less weight
    Than Aquitaine, a dowry for a queen.
    Be now as prodigal of all dear grace,
    As Nature was in making graces dear,          10
    When she did starve the general world beside,
    And prodigally gave them all to you.
PRIN.   Good Lord Boyet, my beauty, though but mean,
    Needs not the painted flourish of your praise:
    Beauty is bought by judgment of the eye,
    Not utter'd by base sale of chapmen's tongues:
    I am less proud to hear you tell my worth
    Than you much willing to be counted wise
    In spending your wit in the praise of mine.
    But now to task the tasker: good Boyet,        20
    You are not ignorant, all-telling fame
    Doth noise abroad, Navarre hath made a vow,
    Till painful study shall outwear three years,
    No woman may approach his silent court:
    Therefore to 's seemeth it a needful course,
    Before we enter his forbidden gates,
    To know his pleasure; and in that behalf,

15

Bold of your worthiness, we single you
As our best-moving fair solicitor.
Tell him, the daughter of the King of France, 30
On serious business craving quick dispatch,
Importunes personal conference with his Grace:
Haste, signify so much; while we attend,
Like humble-visaged suitors, his high will.

BOYET.    Proud of employment, willingly I go.

PRIN.    All pride is willing pride, and yours is so.    [*Exit* BOYET.
Who are the votaries, my loving lords,
That are vow-fellows with this virtuous duke?

FIRST LORD.    Lord Longaville is one.

PRIN.                                        Know you the man? 40

MAR.    I know him, madam: at a marriage-feast,
Between Lord Perigort and the beauteous heir
Of Jaques Falconbridge, solemnized
In Normandy, saw I this Longaville:
A man of sovereign parts he is esteem'd;
Well fitted in arts, glorious in arms:
Nothing becomes him ill that he would well.
The only soil of his fair virtue's gloss,
If virtue's gloss will stain with any soil,
Is a sharp wit match'd with too blunt a will; 50
Whose edge hath power to cut, whose will still wills
It should none spare that come within his power.

PRIN.    Some merry mocking lord, belike; is 't so?

MAR.    They say so most that most his humours know.

PRIN.    Such short-lived wits do wither as they grow.
Who are the rest?

KATH.    The young Dumain, a well-accomplish'd youth,
Of all that virtue love for virtue loved:
Most power to do most harm, least knowing ill;
For he hath wit to make an ill shape good, 60
And shape to win grace, though he had no wit.
I saw him at the Duke Alençon's once;
And much too little of that good I saw
Is my report to his great worthiness.

ROS.    Another of these students at that time
Was there with him, if I have heard a truth.

---

28 *Bold*] Confident.
43 *Jaques*] A dissyllable, with the accent on the first syllable: *solemnized* is here a quadri-
    syllable, with accents on the second and fourth syllables.
58 *Of all . . . loved*] Loved for virtue by all those who have regard for virtue.

    Biron they call him; but a merrier man,
    Within the limit of becoming mirth,
    I never spent an hour's talk withal:
    His eye begets occasion for his wit;     70
    For every object that the one doth catch,
    The other turns to a mirth-moving jest,
    Which his fair tongue, conceit's expositor,
    Delivers in such apt and gracious words,
    That aged ears play truant at his tales,
    And younger hearings are quite ravished;
    So sweet and voluble is his discourse.
PRIN.    God bless my ladies! are they all in love,
    That every one her own hath garnished
    With such bedecking ornaments of praise?     80
FIRST LORD.    Here comes Boyet.

*Re-enter* BOYET

PRIN.                  Now, what admittance, lord?
BOYET.    Navarre had notice of your fair approach;
    And he and his competitors in oath
    Were all address'd to meet you, gentle lady,
    Before I came. Marry, thus much I have learnt:
    He rather means to lodge you in the field,
    Like one that comes here to besiege his court,
    Than seek a dispensation for his oath,
    To let you enter his unpeeled house.     90
    Here comes Navarre.

*Enter* KING, LONGAVILLE, DUMAIN, BIRON, *and* Attendants

KING.    Fair princess, welcome to the court of Navarre.
PRIN.    "Fair" I give you back again; and "welcome" I have not
    yet: the roof of this court is too high to be yours; and wel-
    come to the wide fields too base to be mine.
KING.    You shall be welcome, madam, to my court.
PRIN.    I will be welcome, then: conduct me thither.
KING.    Hear me, dear lady; I have sworn an oath.
PRIN.    Our Lady help my lord! he'll be forsworn.
KING.    Not for the world, fair madam, by my will.     100
PRIN.    Why, will shall break it; will, and nothing else.

70 *begets*] in the sense of "procures."
100–101 *will . . . will*] A quibble on two of the varied contemporary meanings of "will,"
    which in line 100 is used synonymously with "free consent," as in "willingly," and
    in line 101, with the equally common signification of "sensual desire." In line 215
    "will" is used in the sense of "strength of will," or resolve.

KING. Your ladyship is ignorant what it is.
PRIN. Were my lord so, his ignorance were wise,
    Where now his knowledge must prove ignorance.
    I hear your grace hath sworn out house-keeping:
    'T is deadly sin to keep that oath, my lord,
    And sin to break it.
    But pardon me, I am too sudden-bold:
    To teach a teacher ill beseemeth me.
    Vouchsafe to read the purpose of my coming,     110
    And suddenly resolve me in my suit.
KING. Madam, I will, if suddenly I may.
PRIN. You will the sooner, that I were away;
    For you'll prove perjured, if you make me stay.
BIRON. Did not I dance with you in Brabant once?
ROS. Did not I dance with you in Brabant once?
BIRON. I know you did.
ROS. How needless was it, then, to ask the question!
BIRON. You must not be so quick.
ROS. 'T is 'long of you that spur me with such questions.     120
BIRON. Your wit 's too hot, it speeds too fast, 't will tire.
ROS. Not till it leave the rider in the mire.
BIRON. What time o' day?
ROS. The hour that fools should ask.
BIRON. Now fair befall your mask!
ROS. Fair fall the face it covers!
BIRON. And send you many lovers!
ROS. Amen, so you be none.
BIRON. Nay, then will I be gone.
KING. Madam, your father here doth intimate     130
    The payment of a hundred thousand crowns;
    Being but the one half of an entire sum
    Disbursed by my father in his wars.
    But say that he or we, as neither have,
    Received that sum, yet there remains unpaid
    A hundred thousand more; in surety of the which,

131 *a hundred thousand crowns*] Hunter first pointed out an authentic incident in fifteenth-century French history which somewhat resembles the negotiation described in this speech. Before his death in 1425, according to Monstrelet's Chronicle, Charles, King of Navarre, surrendered certain lands to Charles VII, King of France, in exchange for certain other lands and the payment of *two hundred thousand crowns*. In the play the hero is the son of the King of Navarre who made this bargain, and he claims the payment in full of the *two hundred thousand crowns*. The princess asserts that the whole debt is already discharged. Shakespeare very liberally adapts the historic episode to his dramatic purpose.

One part of Aquitaine is bound to us,
Although not valued to the money's worth.
If, then, the king your father will restore
But that one-half which is unsatisfied,                    140
We will give up our right in Aquitaine,
And hold fair friendship with his Majesty.
But that, it seems, he little purposeth,
For here he doth demand to have repaid
A hundred thousand crowns; and not demands,
On payment of a hundred thousand crowns,
To have his title live in Aquitaine;
Which we much rather had depart withal,
And have the money by our father lent,
Than Aquitaine so gelded as it is.                         150
Dear princess, were not his requests so far
From reason's yielding, your fair self should make
A yielding 'gainst some reason, in my breast,
And go well satisfied to France again.

PRIN.    You do the king my father too much wrong,
And wrong the reputation of your name,
In so unseeming to confess receipt
Of that which hath so faithfully been paid.

KING.    I do protest I never heard of it;
And if you prove it, I'll repay it back,                   160
Or yield up Aquitaine.

PRIN.                          We arrest your word.
Boyet, you can produce acquittances
For such a sum from special officers
Of Charles his father.

KING.                          Satisfy me so.

BOYET.    So please your Grace, the packet is not come,
Where that and other specialties are bound:
To-morrow you shall have a sight of them.

KING.    It shall suffice me: at which interview          170
All liberal reason I will yield unto.
Meantime receive such welcome at my hand
As honour, without breach of honour, may
Make tender of to thy true worthiness:
You may not come, fair princess, in my gates;
But here without you shall be so received
As you shall deem yourself lodged in my heart,
Though so denied fair harbour in my house.
Your own good thoughts excuse me, and farewell:

To-morrow shall we visit you again.                                    180
PRIN.  Sweet health and fair desires consort your Grace!
KING.  Thy own wish wish I thee in every place!            [*Exit.*
BIRON.  Lady, I will commend you to mine own heart.
ROS.  Pray you, do my commendations; I would be glad to see
     it.
BIRON.  I would you heard it grown
ROS.  Is the fool sick?
BIRON.  Sick at the heart.
ROS.  Alack, let it blood.
BIRON.  Would that do it good?                                         190
ROS.  My physics say "ay."
BIRON.  Will you prick 't with your eye?
ROS.  No point, with my knife.
BIRON.  Now, God save thy life!
ROS.  And yours from long living!
BIRON.  I cannot stay thanksgiving.                        [*Retiring.*
DUM.  Sir, I pray you, a word: what lady is that same?
BOYET.  The heir of Alençon, Katharine her name.
DUM.  A gallant lady. Monsieur, fare you well.             [*Exit.*
LONG.  I beseech you a word: what is she in the white?                 200
BOYET.  A woman sometimes, an you saw her in the light.
LONG.  Perchance light in the light. I desire her name.
BOYET.  She hath but one for herself, to desire that were a
     shame.
LONG.  Pray you, sir, whose daughter?
BOYET.  Her mother's I have heard.
LONG.  God's blessing on your beard!
BOYET.  Good sir, be not offended.
     She is an heir of Falconbridge.
LONG.  Nay, my choler is ended.
     She is a most sweet lady.                                         210
BOYET.  Not unlike, sir, that may be.                      [*Exit* LONG.
BIRON.  What's her name in the cap?
BOYET.  Rosaline, by good hap.
BIRON.  Is she wedded or no?
BOYET.  To her will, sir, or so.

---

193 *No point*] A play on the French negative particle. Cf. Cotgrave, *Fr.-Engl. Dict.*,
    1611: "*Point*, an adverbe, not, no one jote, by no meanes, in no manner, not at all."
    Characters speaking broken English on the Elizabethan stage freely used "no
    point" for "no."
202 *light in the light*] wanton in the light.
215 *To her will*] see note on lines 100–101.

BIRON.    You are welcome, sir: adieu.

BOYET.    Farewell to me, sir, and welcome to you.

                                        [*Exit* BIRON.

MAR.    That last is Biron, the merry mad-cap lord:
    Not a word with him but a jest.

BOYET.                              And every jest but a word.        220

PRIN.    It was well done of you to take him at his word.

BOYET.    I was as willing to grapple as he was to board.

MAR.    Two hot sheeps, marry.

BOYET.                              And wherefore not ships?
    No sheep, sweet lamb, unless we feed on your lips.

MAR.    You sheep, and I pasture: shall that finish the jest?

BOYET.    So you grant pasture for me.        [*Offering to kiss her.*

MAR.                              Not so, gentle beast:
    My lips are no common, though several they be.

BOYET.    Belonging to whom?                                        230

MAR.                              To my fortunes and me.

PRIN.    Good wits will be jangling; but, gentles, agree:
    This civil war of wits were much better used
    On Navarre and his book-men; for here 't is abused.

BOYET.    If my observation, which very seldom lies,
    By the heart's still rhetoric disclosed with eyes,
    Deceive me not now, Navarre is infected.

PRIN.    With what?

BOYET.    With that which we lovers entitle affected.

PRIN.    Your reason?                                              240

BOYET.    Why, all his behaviours did make their retire
    To the court of his eye, peeping thorough desire;
    His heart, like an agate, with your print impress'd,
    Proud with his form, in his eye pride express'd:
    His tongue, all impatient to speak and not see,
    Did stumble with haste in his eyesight to be;
    All senses to that sense did make their repair,

223–224 *sheeps . . . ships*] "Sheep" in Elizabethan English was pronounced "ship," as it often is in provincial English nowadays. (The *Ship* Street of Oxford and of other inland English cities was originally *Sheep* Street). Boyet's query naturally issues from the nautical figure of "grapple" and "board" in his previous remark.

229 *My lips . . . be*] Maria jests carelessly with familiar legal terms—"common," or land in public or common ownership, and "several," or land in private or separate ownership—which the mention of "pasture" suggests. Maria says punningly that her lips are not common land open for everybody to pasture; though they are more than one (*i.e.* several), they constitute a private or separate domain.

243 *like an agate*] Little figures were often carved on agates set in rings or brooches.

245 *all impatient . . . see*] Thoroughly angry at only being able to speak, and at being unable to perform the function of eyes.

To feel only looking on fairest of fair:
Methought all his senses were lock'd in his eye,
As jewels in crystal for some prince to buy;                    250
Who, tendering their own worth from where they were
    glass'd,
Did point you to buy them, along as you pass'd:
His face's own margent did quote such amazes,
That all eyes saw his eyes enchanted with gazes.
I'll give you Aquitaine, and all that is his,
An you give him for my sake but one loving kiss.

PRIN.    Come to our pavilion: Boyet is disposed.

BOYET.    But to speak that in words which his eye hath disclosed.
I only have made a mouth of his eye,
By adding a tongue which I know will not lie.                    260

ROS.    Thou art an old love-monger, and speakest skilfully.

MAR.    He is Cupid's grandfather, and learns news of him.

ROS.    Then was Venus like her mother; for her father is but
    grim.

BOYET.    Do you hear, my mad wenches?

MAR.               No.

BOYET.               What then, do you see?

ROS.    Ay, our way to be gone.

BOYET.               You are too hard for me.

                                     [*Exeunt.*

---

253 *margent*] In *Rom. and Jul.*, I, iii, 81–92, a lover's face is likened to a volume with
    comments "written in the margent of his eyes." The margins of books were often
    crowded with illustrative quotations.
257 *disposed*] *sc.* to merriment, as *infra*, V, ii, 494.

# ACT III.

## Scene I. *The Same.*

*Enter* ARMADO *and* MOTH

ARMADO.  Warble, child; make passionate my sense of hearing.

MOTH.  Concolinel.                                                 [*Singing.*

ARM.  Sweet air! Go, tenderness of years; take this key, give enlargement to the swain, bring him festinately hither: I must employ him in a letter to my love.

MOTH.  Master, will you win your love with a French brawl?

ARM.  How meanest thou? brawling in French?

MOTH.  No, my complete master: but to jig off a tune at the tongue's end, canary to it with your feet, humour it with turning up your eyelids, sigh a note and sing a note, some-    10
time through the throat, as if you swallowed love with singing love, sometime through the nose, as if you snuffed up love by smelling love; with your hat penthouse-like o'er the shop of your eyes; with your arms crossed on your thin-belly doublet, like a rabbit on a spit; or your hands in your pocket, like a man after the old painting; and keep not too long in one tune, but a snip and away. These are complements, these are humours; these betray nice wenches, that would be betrayed without these; and make them men of note—do you note me?—that most are affected to these    20

2 *Concolinel*] Probably the refrain of the song sung by Moth. The sound of the word, coupled with the reference to a *French* brawl at line 6, suggests that the song was French. The word may be a corruption of "quand colinelle." Far-fetched endeavours have been made to identify it with an Irish air,—"Callen o Custure me,"—which is frequently mentioned in Elizabethan literature, and is quoted by Pistol in *Hen.* V, IV, iv, 4.

6 *a French brawl*] a French dance resembling a cotillon.

9 *canary*] dance the lively Spanish dance, which owed its name to the belief that it was derived from the aborigines of the Canary Islands.

13 *penthouse-like*] like an overhanging or projecting roof over a shop window.

23

ARM. How hast thou purchased this experience?

MOTH. By my penny of observation.

ARM. But O,—but O,—

MOTH. "The hobby-horse is forgot."

ARM. Callest thou my love "hobby-horse"?

MOTH. No, master; the hobby-horse is but a colt, and your love perhaps a hackney. But have you forgot your love?

ARM. Almost I had.

MOTH. Negligent student! learn her by heart.

ARM. By heart and in heart, boy.      30

MOTH. And out of heart, master: all those three I will prove.

ARM. What wilt thou prove?

MOTH. A man, if I live; and this, by, in, and without, upon the instant: by heart you love her, because your heart cannot come by her; in heart you love her, because your heart is in love with her; and out of heart you love her, being out of heart that you cannot enjoy her.

ARM. I am all these three.

MOTH. And three times as much more, and yet nothing at all.

ARM. Fetch hither the swain: he must carry me a letter.    40

MOTH. A message well sympathized; a horse to be ambassador for an ass.

ARM. Ha, ha! what sayest thou?

MOTH. Marry, sir, you must send the ass upon the horse, for he is very slow-gaited. But I go.

ARM. The way is but short: away!

MOTH. As swift as lead, sir.

ARM. The meaning, pretty ingenious?
Is not lead a metal heavy, dull, and slow?

MOTH. Minimè, honest master; or rather, master, no.    50

ARM. I say lead is slow.

MOTH.                You are too swift, sir, to say so:
Is that lead slow which is fired from a gun?

ARM. Sweet smoke of rhetoric!
He reputes me a cannon; and the bullet, that's he:
I shoot thee at the swain.

---

24 *"The hobby-horse is forgot"*] Doubtless a quotation from a popular song lamenting the decay, under Puritan influence, of May-day or morris dances, in which the "hobby-horse"—a man or boy with a wicker frame resembling a horse's body fastened about his waist—played a prominent part. The phrase is often found in the Elizabethan dramatists.

26–27 *the hobby-horse . . . hackney*] "Hobby-horse" and "hackney" were both terms applied to a woman of loose character. "Colt" is here used in the sense of "lascivious fellow."

MOTH.                           Thump, then, and I flee.     [*Exit.*
ARM.     A most acute juvenal; volable and free of grace!
    By thy favour, sweet welkin, I must sigh in thy face:
    Most rude melancholy, valour gives thee place.                    70
    My herald is return'd.

*Re-enter* MOTH *with* COSTARD

MOTH.    A wonder, master! here's a Costard broken in a shin.
ARM.     Some enigma, some riddle: come, thy l'envoy; begin.
COST.    No egma, no riddle, no l'envoy; no salve in the mail, sir:
    O, sir, plantain, a plain plantain! no l'envoy, no l'envoy; no
    salve, sir, but a plantain!
ARM.     By virtue, thou enforcest laughter; thy silly thought my
    spleen; the heaving of my lungs provokes me to ridiculous
    smiling. O, pardon me, my stars! Doth the inconsiderate
    take salve for l'envoy, and the word l'envoy for a salve?          80
MOTH.    Do the wise think them other? is not l'envoy a salve?
ARM.     No, page: it is an epilogue or discourse, to make plain
    Some obscure precedence that hath tofore been sain.
    I will example it:
        The fox, the ape, and the humble-bee,
        Were still at odds, being but three.
    There's the moral. Now the l'envoy.
MOTH.    I will add the l'envoy. Say the moral again.
ARM.         The fox, the ape, the humble-bee,
        Were still at odds, being but three.                             90
MOTH.        Until the goose came out of door,
        And stay'd the odds by adding four.
    Now will I begin your moral, and do you follow with my
    l'envoy.
        The fox, the ape, and the humble-bee,
        Were still at odds, being but three.
ARM.         Until the goose came out of door,
        Staying the odds by adding four.

---

74 *no salve in the mail*] no curative ointment in the boy's wallet, or pack. The Quartos
    and First Folio read obscurely *in thee male*, for which the Second Folio substituted
    *in the male* (*i.e.*, mail, budget, wallet). Malone adopted the reading which is adopted
    here. Perhaps a simpler change would be *in them all*.
81 *l'envoy a salve*] "Envoy" is the concluding stanza of a ballade or short poem, and
    often took the form of a propitiatory address to a patron. Here it implies unctuous
    flattery. There is a quibble on the meaning of *salve*, which stands both for a "cura-
    tive ointment" and the Latin greeting of welcome and farewell.

MOTH.    A good l'envoy, ending in the goose: would you desire
more?                                                    100

COST.    The boy hath sold him a bargain, a goose that's flat.
Sir, your pennyworth is good, an your goose be fat.
To sell a bargain well is as cunning as fast and loose:
Let me see; a fat l'envoy; ay, that's a fat goose.

ARM.    Come hither, come hither. How did this argument begin?

MOTH.    By saying that a Costard was broken in a shin.
Then call'd you for the l'envoy.

COST.    True, and I for a plantain: thus came your argument in;
Then the boy's fat l'envoy, the goose that you bought;
And he ended the market.                             110

ARM.    But tell me; how was there a Costard broken in a shin?

MOTH.    I will tell you sensibly.

COST.    Thou hast no feeling of it, Moth: I will speak that
l'envoy:
        I Costard, running out, that was safely within,
        Fell over the threshold, and broke my shin.

ARM.    We will talk no more of this matter.

COST.    Till there be more matter in the shin.

ARM.    Sirrah Costard, I will enfranchise thee.

COST.    O, marry me to one Frances: I smell some l'envoy, some    120
goose, in this.

ARM.    By my sweet soul, I mean setting thee at liberty, enfree-
doming thy person: thou wert immured, restrained, capti-
vated, bound.

COST.    True, true; and now you will be my purgation, and let
me loose.

ARM.    I give thee thy liberty, set thee from durance; and, in lieu
thereof, impose on thee nothing but this: bear this signifi-
cant [*giving a letter*] to the country maid Jaquenetta: there is
remuneration; for the best ward of mine honour is rewarding    130
my dependents. Moth, follow.                             [*Exit.*

MOTH.    Like the sequel, I. Signior Costard, adieu.

COST.    My sweet ounce of man's flesh! my incony Jew!
                                      [*Exit* MOTH.
Now will I look to his remuneration. Remuneration! O,
that's the Latin word for three farthings: three farthings—remuneration.—"What's the price of this inkle?"—"One
penny."—"No, I'll give you a remuneration:" why, it carries

101 *sold him a bargain*] made a fool of him.
103 *fast and loose*] See note *supra*, I, ii, 140.
133 *Jew*] Probably a colloquial abbreviation of jewel.

it. Remuneration! why, it is a fairer name than French
crown. I will never buy and sell out of this word.

*Enter* BIRON

BIRON.    O, my good knave Costard! exceedingly well met.        140
COST.    Pray you, sir, how much carnation ribbon may a man
    buy for a remuneration?
BIRON.    What is a remuneration?
COST.    Marry, sir, halfpenny farthing.
BIRON.    Why, then, three-farthing worth of silk.
COST.    I thank your worship: God be wi' you!
BIRON.    Stay, slave; I must employ thee:
    As thou wilt win my favour, good my knave,
    Do one thing for me that I shall entreat.
COST.    When would you have it done, sir?                       150
BIRON.    This afternoon.
COST.    Well, I will do it, sir: fare you well.
BIRON.    Thou knowest not what it is.
COST.    I shall know, sir, when I have done it.
BIRON.    Why, villain, thou must know first.
COST.    I will come to your worship to-morrow morning.
BIRON.    It must be done this afternoon. Hark, slave, it is but this:
    The princess comes to hunt here in the park,
    And in her train there is a gentle lady;
    When tongues speak sweetly, then they name her name,    160
    And Rosaline they call her: ask for her;
    And to her white hand see thou do commend
    This seal'd-up counsel. There's thy guerdon; go.
                            *[Giving him a shilling.*
COST.    Gardon, O sweet gardon! better than remuneration, a
    'leven-pence farthing better: most sweet gardon! I will do it,
    sir, in print. Gardon! Remuneration!            *[Exit.*
BIRON.    And I, forsooth, in love! I, that have been love's whip;
    A very beadle to a humorous sigh;
    A critic, nay, a night-watch constable;
    A domineering pedant o'er the boy;                      170
    Than whom no mortal so magnificent!

138–139 *French crown*] The slang term for venereal disease, which produced baldness.
163 *guerdon*] In a tract *A health to the gentlemanly profession of serving men*, by I. M.,
    which was published in 1598, there is the same anecdote of a servant receiving from
    one patron three farthings, which he calls *remuneration*, and from another patron
    a shilling, which he calls *guerdon*. The pamphleteer was probably echoing
    Shakespeare.
168 *beadle*] A beadle's functions included that of whipping offenders.

This wimpled, whining, purblind, wayward boy;
This senior-junior, giant-dwarf, Dan Cupid;
Regent of love-rhymes, lord of folded arms,
The anointed sovereign of sighs and groans,
Liege of all loiterers and malcontents,
Dread prince of plackets, king of codpieces,
Sole imperator and great general
Of trotting 'paritors:—O my little heart!—
And I to be a corporal of his field,                                      180
And wear his colours like a tumbler's hoop!
What! I love! I sue! I seek a wife!
A woman, that is like a German clock,
Still a-repairing, ever out of frame,
And never going aright, being a watch,
But being watch'd that it may still go right!
Nay, to be perjured, which is worst of all;
And, among three, to love the worst of all;
A whitely wanton with a velvet brow,
With two pitch-balls stuck in her face for eyes;          190
Ay, and, by heaven, one that will do the deed,
Though Argus were her eunuch and her guard:
And I to sigh for her! to watch for her!
To pray for her! Go to; it is a plague
That Cupid will impose for my neglect
Of his almighty dreadful little might.
Well, I will love, write, sigh, pray, sue and groan:
Some men must love my lady, and some Joan.          [*Exit.*

---

177 *plackets . . . codpieces*] men and women, from distinctive features of their attire.
181 *colours . . . hoop*] A tumbler's hoop was ornamented with coloured ribbons.
189 *whitely*] The first Quarto and First Folio read *whitly*, which stands apparently for
   "whitely," *i.e.*, whitish pale, pasty-faced. The epithet does not seem very appropriate
   to the dark complexion, with which Biron's lady love is credited. The suggested
   reading *wightly*, *i.e.*, witchlike, freakish, nimble, is worth considering.

# ACT IV.

## SCENE I. *The Same.*

*Enter the* PRINCESS, *and her train, a* FORESTER, BOYET,
ROSALINE, MARIA, *and* KATHARINE

PRINCESS.   Was that the King, that spurr'd his horse so hard
    Against the steep uprising of the hill?
BOYET.   I know not; but I think it was not he.
PRIN.   Whoe'er a' was, a' showed a mounting mind.
    Well, lords, to-day we shall have our dispatch:
    On Saturday we will return to France.
    Then, forester, my friend, where is the bush
    That we must stand and play the murderer in?
FOR.   Hereby, upon the edge of yonder coppice;
    A stand where you may make the fairest shoot.     10
PRIN.   I thank my beauty, I am fair that shoot,
    And thereupon thou speak'st the fairest shoot.
FOR.   Pardon me, madam, for I meant not so.
PRIN.   What, what? first praise me, and again say no?
    O short-lived pride! Not fair? alack for woe!
FOR.   Yes, madam, fair.
PRIN.                   Nay, never paint me now:
    Where fair is not, praise cannot mend the brow.
    Here, good my glass, take this for telling true:
    Fair payment for foul words is more than due.     20
FOR.   Nothing but fair is that which you inherit.
PRIN.   See, see, my beauty will be saved by merit!
    O heresy in fair, fit for these days!
    A giving hand, though foul, shall have fair praise.
    But come, the bow: now mercy goes to kill,

---

10 *stand*] A technical term in hunting for the huntsmen's station or hiding-place in the
    bushes, from which he takes aim at the quarry.

And shooting well is then accounted ill.
Thus will I save my credit in the shoot:
Not wounding, pity would not let me do 't;
If wounding, then it was to show my skill,
That more for praise than purpose meant to kill.      30
And, out of question, so it is sometimes,
Glory grows guilty of detested crimes,
When, for fame's sake, for praise, an outward part,
We bend to that the working of the heart;
As I for praise alone now seek to spill
The poor deer's blood, that my heart means no ill.
BOYET.    Do not curst wives hold that self-sovereignty
     Only for praise sake, when they strive to be
     Lords o'er their lords?
PRIN.    Only for praise: and praise we may afford      40
     To any lady that subdues a lord.
BOYET.    Here comes a member of the commonwealth.

*Enter* COSTARD

COST.    God dig-you-den all! Pray you, which is the head lady?
PRIN.    Thou shalt know her, fellow, by the rest that have no
     heads.
COST.    Which is the greatest lady, the highest?
PRIN.    The thickest and the tallest.
COST.    The thickest and the tallest! it is so; truth is truth.
     An your waist, mistress, were as slender as my wit,
     One o' these maids' girdles for your waist should be fit.      50
     Are not you the chief woman? you are the thickest here.
PRIN.    What's your will, sir? what's your will?
COST.    I have a letter from Monsieur Biron to one Lady
     Rosaline.
PRIN.    O, thy letter, thy letter! he's a good friend of mine:
     Stand aside, good bearer. Boyet, you can carve;
     Break up this capon.
BOYET.                  I am bound to serve.
     This letter is mistook, it importeth none here;
     It is writ to Jaquenetta.

37–39 *Do not curst wives . . . lords?*] Do not shrewish wives regard the display of self-
control merely as a pretence, as a way of winning the good opinion of onlookers,
while they are striving to bring their husbands into subjection?
56 *capon*] love-letter, in the sense of the French "pullet." Cf. Cotgrave, *Fr.-Engl. Dict.*:
"*Pullet*, a chicken, also a love letter or love message." "Break up" was often used in
the sense of "carve."

PRIN.                    We will read it, I swear.                          60
    Break the neck of the wax, and every one give ear.
BOYET [*reads*].   By heaven, that thou art fair, is most infallible; true,
    that thou art beauteous; truth itself, that thou art lovely. More fairer
    than fair, beautiful than beauteous, truer than truth itself, have
    commiseration on thy heroical vassal! The magnanimous and most
    illustrate king Cophetua set eye upon the pernicious and indubi-
    tate beggar Zenelophon; and he it was that might rightly say, Veni,
    vidi, vici; which to annothanize in the vulgar,—O base and ob-
    scure vulgar!—videlicet, He came, saw, and overcame: he came,
    one; saw, two; overcame, three. Who came? the king: why did he     70
    come? to see: why did he see? to overcome: to whom came he? to
    the beggar: what saw he? the beggar: who overcame he? the beg-
    gar. The conclusion is victory: on whose side? the king's. The cap-
    tive is enriched: on whose side? the beggar's. The catastrophe is a
    nuptial: on whose side? the king's: no, on both in one, or one in
    both. I am the king; for so stands the comparison: thou the beggar;
    for so witnesseth thy lowliness. Shall I command thy love? I may:
    shall I enforce thy love? I could: shall I entreat thy love? I will.
    What shalt thou exchange for rags? robes; for tittles? titles; for thy-
    self? me. Thus, expecting thy reply, I profane my lips on thy foot,    80
    my eyes on thy picture, and my heart on thy every part. Thine, in
    the dearest design of industry,          DON ADRIANO DE ARMADO.
        Thus dost thou hear the Nemean lion roar
           'Gainst thee, thou lamb, that standest as his prey.
        Submissive fall his princely feet before,
           And he from forage will incline to play:
        But if thou strive, poor soul, what art thou then?
        Food for his rage, repasture for his den.
PRIN.   What plume of feathers is he that indited this letter?
    What vane? what weathercock? did you ever hear better?             90
BOYET.   I am much deceived but I remember the style.
PRIN.   Else your memory is bad, going o'er it erewhile.
BOYET.   This Armado is a Spaniard, that keeps here in court;
    A phantasime, a Monarcho, and one that makes sport
    To the prince and his bookmates.

---

66 *Cophetua*] See note *supra*, I, ii, 98. In the ballad the beggar's name is given as
    "Penelophon."
94 *a Monarcho*] A half-witted Italian, who frequented Queen Elizabeth's court at this
    period, was known by this name. Thomas Churchyard in his poetic miscellany, A
    *pleasaunte Laborinth called Churchyardes Chance* (1596), has a poem, headed "The
    Phantasticall *Monarkes* Epitaphe," which quaintly describes the man's pompous
    speech and carriage. According to Reginald Scot's *Discoverie of Witchcraft*, 1584,
    p. 54, "the Italian whom we call in England *the Monarch*" laboured under the delu-
    sion that he owned all the ships arriving in the port of London.

PRIN.                                       Thou fellow, a word:
   Who gave thee this letter?
COST.                            I told you; my lord.
PRIN.    To whom shouldst thou give it?
COST.                                From my lord to my lady.    100
PRIN.    From which lord to which lady?
COST.    From my lord Biron, a good master of mine,
   To a lady of France that he call'd Rosaline.
PRIN.    Thou hast mistaken his letter. Come, lords, away.
   [*To* ROS.] Here, sweet, put up this: 't will be thine another
            day.                           [*Exeunt* PRINCESS *and train.*
BOYET.    Who is the suitor? who is the suitor?
ROS.                            Shall I teach you to know?
BOYET.    Ay, my continent of beauty.
ROS.                            Why, she that bears the bow.
   Finely put off!                                              110
BOYET.    My lady goes to kill horns; but, if thou marry,
   Hang me by the neck, if horns that year miscarry.
   Finely put on!
ROS.    Well, then, I am the shooter.
BOYET.                            And who is your deer?
ROS.    If we choose by the horns, yourself come not near.
   Finely put on, indeed!
MAR.    You still wrangle with her, Boyet, and she strikes at the
            brow.
BOYET.    But she herself is hit lower: have I hit her now?
ROS.    Shall I come upon thee with an old saying, that was a man    120
   when King Pepin of France was a little boy, as touching the
   hit it?
BOYET.    So I may answer thee with one as old, that was a woman
   when Queen Guinover of Britain was a little wench, as
   touching the hit it.
ROS.                      Thou canst not hit it, hit it, hit it,
                          Thou canst not hit it, my good man.
BOYET.                    An I cannot, cannot, cannot,
                          An I cannot, another can.
                                       [*Exeunt* ROS. *and* KATH.
COST.    By my troth, most pleasant: how both did fit it!          130
MAR.    A mark marvellous well shot, for they both did hit it.

---

106 *suitor*] All the early copies read *Shooter*, which Steevens first changed to *suitor*. The
   verbal quips which follow depend on the similarity in pronunciation of these two
   words.

BOYET.    A mark! O, mark but that mark! A mark, says my lady!
    Let the mark have a prick in 't, to mete at, if it may be.
MAR.    Wide o' the bow-hand! i' faith, your hand is out.
COST.    Indeed, a' must shoot nearer, or he'll ne'er hit the clout.
BOYET.    An if my hand be out, then belike your hand is in.
COST.    Then will she get the upshoot by cleaving the pin.
MAR.    Come, come, you talk greasily; your lips grow foul.
COST.    She's too hard for you at pricks, sir: challenge her to
    bowl.
BOYET.    I fear too much rubbing. Good night, my good owl.          140
                                [*Exeunt* BOYET *and* MARIA.
COST.    By my soul, a swain! a most simple clown!
    Lord, Lord, how the ladies and I have put him down!
    O' my troth, most sweet jests! most incony vulgar wit!
    When it comes so smoothly off, so obscenely, as it were, so
      fit.
    Armado o' th' one side,—O, a most dainty man!
    To see him walk before a lady and to bear her fan!
    To see him kiss his hand! and how most sweetly a' will swear!
    And his page o' t' other side, that handful of wit!
    Ah, heavens, it is a most pathetical nit!
    Sola, sola!                                         [*Shout within.*    150
                               [*Exit* COSTARD, *running.*

## SCENE II. *The Same.*

*Enter* HOLOFERNES, SIR NATHANIEL, *and* DULL

NATH.    Very reverend sport, truly; and done in the testimony of
    a good conscience.
HOL.    The deer was, as you know, sanguis, in blood; ripe as the
    pomewater, who now hangeth like a jewel in the ear of
    caelo, the sky, the welkin, the heaven; and anon falleth like
    a crab on the face of terra, the soil, the land, the earth.
NATH.    Truly, Master Holofernes, the epithets are sweetly varied,

---

133–137 *prick . . . clout . . . pin*] These words all refer to the centre or bull's eye of the
    target. The "clout" seems to have been a square white mark, kept in position by a
    "pin" or wooden nail.

---

3 *in blood*] in perfect condition.

　　　like a scholar at the least: but, sir, I assure ye, it was a buck
　　　of the first head.

HOL.　　Sir Nathaniel, *haud credo.*　　　　　　　　　　　　　10

DULL.　'T was not a *haud credo;* 't was a pricket.

HOL.　　Most barbarous intimation! yet a kind of insinuation, as it
　　　were, in via, in way, of explication; *facere,* as it were, replica-
　　　tion, or, rather, *ostentare,* to show, as it were, his inclination,
　　　after his undressed, unpolished, uneducated, unpruned, un-
　　　trained, or, rather, unlettered, or, ratherest, unconfirmed
　　　fashion, to insert again my *haud credo* for a deer.

DULL.　I said the deer was not a *haud credo;* 't was a pricket.

HOL.　　Twice-sod simplicity, *bis coctus!*
　　　O thou monster Ignorance, how deformed dost thou look!　20

NATH.　Sir, he hath never fed of the dainties that are bred in a
　　　　　book;
　　　he hath not eat paper, as it were; he hath not drunk ink:
　　　his intellect is not replenished; he is only an animal, only
　　　sensible in the duller parts:
　　　And such barren plants are set before us, that we thankful
　　　　　should be,
　　　Which we of taste and feeling are, for those parts that do
　　　　　fructify in us more than he.
　　　For as it would ill become me to be vain, indiscreet, or a
　　　　　fool,
　　　So were there a patch set on learning, to see him in a school:
　　　But *omne bene,* say I; being of an old father's mind,
　　　Many can brook the weather that love not the wind.　　　30

DULL.　You two are book-men: can you tell me by your wit
　　　What was a month old at Cain's birth, that's not five weeks
　　　　　old as yet?

HOL.　　Dictynna, goodman Dull; Dictynna, goodman Dull.

DULL.　What is Dictynna?

NATH.　A title to Phœbe, to Luna, to the moon.

HOL.　　The moon was a month old when Adam was no more,
　　　And raught not to five weeks when he came to five-score.
　　　The allusion holds in the exchange.

---

8–9 *a buck of the first head*] Here, as in ll. 11, 18, and 44 ("pricket"), ll. 52–56 ("sore"),
　　and ll. 53–55 ("sorel"), allusion is made to the various appellations applied to deer
　　according to their ages. Cf. *The Return from Parnassus,* 1602, ed. Macray, Act II, Sc.
　　v. p. 107: "A Bucke of the first yeare is a fawne; the second yeare, a *Pricket;* the third
　　year, a *Sorell;* the fourth yeare, a *Sore;* the fift, a *Buck of the first head;* the sixt yeare,
　　a compleat Buck."

33 *Dictynna*] A name bestowed by Ovid on Diana.

DULL.   'T is true indeed; the collusion holds in the exchange.

HOL.   God comfort thy capacity! I say, the allusion holds in the      40
exchange.

DULL.   And I say, the pollusion holds in the exchange; for the
moon is never but a month old: and I say beside that, 't was
a pricket that the princess killed.

HOL.   Sir Nathaniel, will you hear an extemporal epitaph on the
death of the deer? And, to humour the ignorant, call I the
deer the princess killed a pricket.

NATH.   Perge, good Master Holofernes, perge; so it shall please
you to abrogate scurrility.

HOL.   I will something affect the letter, for it argues facility.    50

The preyful princess pierced and prick'd a pretty pleasing pricket;
 Some say a sore; but not a sore, till now made sore with shooting.
The dogs did yell: put L to sore, then sorel jumps from thicket;
 Or pricket sore, or else sorel; the people fall a-hooting.
If sore be sore, then L to sore makes fifty sores one sorel.
Of one sore I an hundred make by adding but one more L.

NATH.   A rare talent!

DULL. [*Aside*]   If a talent be a claw, look how he claws him with
a talent.

HOL.   This is a gift that I have, simple, simple; a foolish extra-   60
vagant spirit, full of forms, figures, shapes, objects, ideas,
apprehensions, motions, revolutions: these are begot in
the ventricle of memory, nourished in the womb of pia
mater, and delivered upon the mellowing of occasion. But
the gift is good in those in whom it is acute, and I am thankful for it.

NATH.   Sir, I praise the Lord for you: and so may my parish-
ioners; for their sons are well tutored by you, and their
daughters profit very greatly under you: you are a good
member of the commonwealth.                                           70

HOL.   Mehercle, if their sons be ingenuous, they shall want no
instruction; if their daughters be capable, I will put it to
them: but vir sapit qui pauca loquitur; a soul feminine
saluteth us.

*Enter* JAQUENETTA *and* COSTARD

---

50 *affect the letter*] employ alliteration.

57 *a rare talent*] A play on the words "talent" and "talon." The latter was often spelt "talent." Cf. Nash's *Pierce Pennilesse*, 1595, Sig. F 4: "The Lion without tongue, taile or
*talents*."

JAQ.  God give you good morrow, master Parson.

HOL.  Master Parson, *quasi* pers-on. An if one should be pierced, which is the one?

COST.  Marry, master schoolmaster, he that is likest to a hogshead.

HOL.  Piercing a hogshead! a good lustre of conceit in a turf of 80
earth; fire enough for a flint, pearl enough for a swine: 'tis pretty; it is well.

JAQ.  Good master Parson, be so good as read me this letter: it was given me by Costard, and sent me from Don Armado: I beseech you, read it.

HOL.  *Fauste, precor gelida quando pecus omne sub umbra Ruminat,*—and so forth. Ah, good old Mantuan! I may speak of thee as the traveller doth of Venice;

Venetia, Venetia,

Chi non ti vede non ti pretia. 90

Old Mantuan, old Mantuan! who understandeth thee not, loves thee not. Ut, re, sol, la, mi, fa. Under pardon, sir, what are the contents? or rather, as Horace says in his—What, my soul, verses?

NATH.  Ay, sir, and very learned.

HOL.  Let me hear a staff, a stanze, a verse; *lege, domine.*

NATH. [*reads*]

If love make me forsworn, how shall I swear to love?
Ah, never faith could hold, if not to beauty vow'd!

76–77 *Master Parson . . . the one?*] "Parson" was commonly spelt and pronounced "person." "Pierced" was pronounced "perst"; in New England the surname "Perse" is still pronounced "Pierce." "One" was pronounced "un" or "on."

86–87 *Fauste, precor . . . good old Mantuan*] The Latin words are the opening words of the first of the eclogues of the Latin poet, Baptista Mantuanus (1448–1516). Mantuanus' Latin poetry was popular throughout Europe in the sixteenth century, and his eclogues were widely used as a school book. Shakespeare probably studied them at the grammar school of Stratford-on-Avon. An English translation by George Turberville appeared in 1567, and was reprinted many times.

89–90 *Venetia . . . pretia*] An often quoted Italian proverb ("Venice, Venice, who doth not see thee, doth not value thee"). It appears in James Sandford's *Garden of Pleasure,* 1573, and in John Florio's *First Fruites,* 1578, and in his *Second Flutes,* 1591.

97–110] This sonnet, together with Longaville's sonnet *infra,* IV, iii, 55–68, and Dumain's verses to Katharine in IV, iii, 99–118, are included in Jaggard's poetic miscellany, *The Passionate Pilgrim. By W. Shakespeare,* 1599. They fill respectively the 5th, 3rd, and 16th places in that collection. The promiscuous order in which Jaggard printed these three pieces, coupled with the textual variations, suggest that he did not derive them direct from the printed text of the play, but employed copies which, in accordance with the practice of the time, were circulating in manuscript among collectors of transcripts of contemporary verse. See introduction to Oxford University Press' facsimile of *The Passionate Pilgrim,* 1905.

    Though to myself forsworn, to thee I'll faithful prove;
       Those thoughts to me were oaks, to thee like osiers bow'd.     100
    Study his bias leaves, and makes his book thine eyes,
       Where all those pleasures live that art would comprehend:
    If knowledge be the mark, to know thee shall suffice;
       Well learned is that tongue that well can thee commend
    All ignorant that soul that sees thee without wonder;
       Which is to me some praise that I thy parts admire:
    Thy eye Jove's lightning bears, thy voice his dreadful thunder,
       Which, not to anger bent, is music and sweet fire.
    Celestial as thou art, O, pardon love this wrong,
    That sings heaven's praise with such an earthly tongue.     110

HOL.    You find not the apostrophas, and so miss the accent: let
    me supervise the canzonet. Here are only numbers ratified;
    but, for the elegancy, facility, and golden cadence of poesy,
    caret. Ovidious Naso was the man: and why, indeed, Naso,
    but for smelling out the odoriferous flowers of fancy, the
    jerks of invention? Imitari is nothing: so doth the hound his
    master, the ape his keeper, the tired horse his rider. But,
    damosella virgin, was this directed to you?
JAQ.    Ay, sir, from one Monsieur Biron, one of the strange
    queen's lords.     120
HOL.    I will overglance the superscript: "To the snow-white hand
    of the most beauteous Lady Rosaline." I will look again on the
    intellect of the letter, for the nomination of the party writing
    to the person written unto: "Your ladyship's in all desired em-
    ployment, BIRON." Sir Nathaniel, this Biron is one of the
    votaries with the king; and here he hath framed a letter to a
    sequent of the stranger queen's, which accidentally, or by
    the way of progression, hath miscarried. Trip and go, my
    sweet; deliver this paper into the royal hand of the king: it
    may concern much. Stay not thy compliment; I forgive thy     130
    duty: adieu.
JAQ.    Good Costard, go with me. Sir, God save your life!
COST.    Have with thee, my girl.        [*Exeunt* COST. *and* JAQ.
NATH.    Sir, you have done this in the fear of God, very reli-
    giously; and, as a certain father saith, —

---

117 *tired horse*] Usually explained as "attired with trappings." But from the context and
    from the use of the word in *Sonnet* 1, 5, "The beast that bears me, *tired* with my
    woe," one must infer the simple sense that fatigue in the horse sympathetically re-
    flects that of his rider.

HOL.   Sir, tell not me of the father; I do fear colourable colours. But to return to the verses: did they please you, Sir Nathaniel?

NATH.   Marvellous well for the pen.

HOL.   I do dine to-day at the father's of a certain pupil of mine;     140 where, if, before repast, it shall please you to gratify the table with a grace, I will, on my privilege I have with the parents of the foresaid child or pupil, undertake your ben venuto; where I will prove those verses to be very unlearned, neither savouring of poetry, wit, nor invention: I beseech your society.

NATH.   And thank you too; for society, saith the text, is the happiness of life.

HOL.   And, certes, the text most infallibly concludes it. [*To* DULL] Sir, I do invite you too; you shall not say me nay: pauca verba. Away! the gentles are at their game, and we will     150 to our recreation.              [*Exeunt.*

## SCENE III. *The Same.*

*Enter* BIRON, *with a paper*

BIRON.   The king he is hunting the deer; I am coursing myself: they have pitched a toil; I am toiling in a pitch,—pitch that defiles: defile! a foul word. Well, set thee down, sorrow! for so they say the fool said, and so say I, and I the fool: well proved, wit! By the Lord, this love is as mad as Ajax: it kills sheep; it kills me, I a sheep: well proved again o' my side! I will not love: if I do, hang me; i' faith, I will not. O, but her eye,—by this light, but for her eye, I would not love her; yes, for her two eyes. Well, I do nothing in the world but lie, and lie in my throat. By heaven, I do love: and it hath taught me     10 to rhyme, and to be melancholy; and here is part of my rhyme, and here my melancholy. Well, she hath one o' my sonnets already: the clown bore it, the fool sent it, and the lady hath it: sweet clown, sweeter fool, sweetest lady! By the world, I would not care a pin, if the other three were in. Here comes one with a paper: God give him grace to groan!                             [*Stands aside.*

---

136 *colourable colours*] plausible pretexts or arguments (of papist, priestly Fathers).

1–16] The whole of Biron's speech is in the precise vein of the prose style of Lyly's comedies.

2 *a pitch*] A probable allusion to the dark complexion with which Lady Rosaline is credited.

*Enter the* KING, *with a paper*

KING.  Ay me!

BIRON. [*Aside*]   Shot, by heaven! Proceed, sweet Cupid: thou
    hast thumped him with thy bird-bolt under the left pap. In
    faith, secrets!                                                                   20

KING. [*reads*]

> So sweet a kiss the golden sun gives not
>     To those fresh morning drops upon the rose,
> As thy eye-beams, when their fresh rays have smote
>     The night of dew that on my cheeks down flows:
> Nor shines the silver moon one half so bright
>     Through the transparent bosom of the deep,
> As doth thy face through tears of mine give light;
>     Thou shinest in every tear that I do weep:
> No drop but as a coach doth carry thee;
>     So ridest thou triumphing in my woe.                          30
> Do but behold the tears that swell in me,
>     And they thy glory through my grief will show:
> But do not love thyself; then thou wilt keep
>     My tears for glasses, and still make me weep.
> O queen of queens! how far dost thou excel,
>     No thought can think, nor tongue of mortal tell.

How shall she know my griefs? I'll drop the paper:—
Sweet leaves, shade folly. Who is he comes here?
                                                        [*Steps aside.*

What, Longaville! and reading! listen, ear.

BIRON.   Now, in thy likeness, one more fool appear!                 40

*Enter* LONGAVILLE, *with a paper*

LONG.   Ay me, I am forsworn!

BIRON.   Why, he comes in like a perjure, wearing papers.

KING.   In love, I hope: sweet fellowship in shame!

BIRON.   One drunkard loves another of the name.

LONG.   Am I the first that have been perjured so?

BIRON.   I could put thee in comfort. Not by two that I know:
    Thou makest the triumviry, the corner-cap of society,
    The shape of Love's Tyburn that hangs up simplicity.

---

42 *a perjure, wearing papers*] a perjurer, a part of whose punishment was to stand in a
    public place wearing papers specifying his offence; see *infra*, IV, iii, 123. Cf. Hall's
    *Chronicle*, 59: "He [*i.e.* Cardinal Wolsey] so punyshed periurye with open punysh-
    ment & open papers werynge, that in hys tyme it was lesse vsed."
47–48 *the corner-cap . . . Tyburn*] the old-fashioned three-cornered hat. The gallows at
    Tyburn were in the form of a triangle.

LONG.   I fear these stubborn lines lack power to move.
  O sweet Maria, empress of my love!          50
  These numbers will I tear, and write in prose.
BIRON.   O, rhymes are guards on wanton Cupid's hose:
  Disfigure not his slop.
LONG.         This same shall go.          [*Reads.*

  Did not the heavenly rhetoric of thine eye,
   'Gainst whom the world cannot hold argument,
  Persuade my heart to this false perjury?
   Vows for thee broke deserve not punishment.
  A woman I forswore; but I will prove,
   Thou being a goddess, I forswore not thee:          60
  My vow was earthly, thou a heavenly love;
   Thy grace being gain'd cures all disgrace in me.
  Vows are but breath, and breath a vapour is:
   Then thou, fair sun, which on my earth dost shine,
  Exhalest this vapour-vow; in thee it is:
   If broken then, it is no fault of mine:
  If by me broke, what fool is not so wise
  To lose an oath to win a paradise?

BIRON.   This is the liver-vein, which makes flesh a deity,
  A green goose a goddess: pure, pure idolatry.          70
  God amend us, God amend! we are much out o' the way.
LONG.   By whom shall I send this?—Company! stay.
           [*Steps aside.*
BIRON.   All hid, all hid, an old infant play.
  Like a demigod here sit I in the sky,
  And wretched fools' secrets heedfully o'er-eye.
  More sacks to the mill! O heavens, I have my wish!

*Enter* DUMAIN, *with a paper*

  Dumain transform'd! four woodcocks in a dish!
DUM.   O most divine Kate!
BIRON.   O most profane coxcomb!
DUM.   By heaven, the wonder in a mortal eye!          80
BIRON.   By earth, she is not, corporal, there you lie.
DUM.   Her amber hairs for foul hath amber quoted.

53 *slop*] wide-kneed breeches, or loose trousers; Theobald's ingenious emendation for
 the meaningless *shop* of the early editions.
55–68] See note on IV, ii, 97–110.
69 *liver-vein*] The liver was commonly held to be the seat of the passion of love. Cf.
 Nashe's *Have with you to Saffron Walden* (1595): "All *liver* am I."
73 *All hid, all hid*] The cry of children playing hide-and-seek.
76 *More sacks to the mill*] A proverb, being a variant of "More grist to the mill."

BIRON.   An amber-colour'd raven was well noted.

DUM.   As upright as the cedar.

BIRON.                                Stoop, I say;
Her shoulder is with child.

DUM.                                As fair as day.

BIRON.   Ay, as some days; but then no sun must shine.

DUM.   O that I had my wish!

LONG.                             And I had mine!                          90

KING.   And I mine too, good Lord!

BIRON.   Amen, so I had mine: is not that a good word?

DUM.   I would forget her; but a fever she
Reigns in my blood, and will remember'd be.

BIRON.   A fever in your blood! why, then incision
Would let her out in saucers: sweet misprision!

DUM.   Once more I'll read the ode that I have writ.

BIRON.   Once more I'll mark how love can vary wit.

DUM. [reads]

> On a day—alack the day!—
> Love, whose month is ever May,                          100
> Spied a blossom passing fair
> Playing in the wanton air:
> Through the velvet leaves the wind,
> All unseen, can passage find;
> That the lover, sick to death,
> Wish himself the heaven's breath.
> Air, quoth he, thy cheeks may blow;
> Air, would I might triumph so!
> But, alack, my hand is sworn
> Ne'er to pluck thee from thy thorn;                     110
> Vow, alack, for youth unmeet,
> Youth so apt to pluck a sweet!
> Do not call it sin in me,
> That I am forsworn for thee;
> Thou for whom Jove would swear
> Juno but an Ethiope were;
> And deny himself for Jove,
> Turning mortal for thy love.

This will I send and something else more plain,
That shall express my true love's fasting pain.          120
O, would the king, Biron, and Longaville,
Were lovers too! Ill, to example ill,

Would from my forehead wipe a perjured note;
For none offend where all alike do dote.

LONG. [*advancing*]    Dumain, thy love is far from charity,
That in love's grief desirest society:
You may look pale, but I should blush, I know,
To be o'erheard and taken napping so.

KING. [*advancing*]    Come, sir, you blush; as his your case is
     such;
You chide at him, offending twice as much;                              130
You do not love Maria; Longaville
Did never sonnet for her sake compile,
Nor never lay his wreathed arms athwart
His loving bosom, to keep down his heart.
I have been closely shrouded in this bush
And mark'd you both and for you both did blush:
I heard your guilty rhymes, observed your fashion,
Saw sighs reek from you, noted well your passion:
Ay me! says one; O Jove! the other cries;
One, her hairs were gold, crystal the other's eyes:                     140
You would for paradise break faith and troth;       [*To* LONG.
And Jove, for your love, would infringe an oath.    [*To* DUM.
What will Biron say when that he shall hear
Faith infringed, which such zeal did swear?
How will he scorn! how will he spend his wit!
How will he triumph, leap and laugh at it!
For all the wealth that ever I did see,
I would not have him know so much by me.

BIRON.    Now step I forth to whip hypocrisy.          [*Advancing*.
Ah, good my liege, I pray thee, pardon me!                              150
Good heart, what grace hast thou, thus to reprove
These worms for loving, that art most in love?
Your eyes do make no coaches; in your tears
There is no certain princess that appears;
You'll not be perjured, 't is a hateful thing;
Tush, none but minstrels like of sonneting!
But are you not ashamed? nay, are you not,
All three of you, to be thus much o'ershot?
You found his mote; the king your mote did see;

---

123 *perjured note*] See note on IV, iii, 42, *supra*.
140 *One, her*] Sidney Walker suggested *One's*, a somewhat more intelligible and metri-
    cally correct reading.
153 *coaches*] reference to the king's sonnet, l. 29, *supra*: "No drop but as a *coach*," etc.
    The old reading is *couches*.

    But I a beam do find in each of three.       160
    O, what a scene of foolery have I seen,
    Of sighs, of groans, of sorrow and of teen!
    O me, with what strict patience have I sat,
    To see a king transformed to a gnat!
    To see great Hercules whipping a gig,
    And profound Solomon to tune a jig,
    And Nestor play at push-pin with the boys,
    And critic Timon laugh at idle toys!
    Where lies thy grief, O, tell me, good Dumain?
    And, gentle Longaville, where lies thy pain?       170
    And where my liege's? all about the breast:
    A caudle, ho!
KING.             Too bitter is thy jest.
    Are we betray'd thus to thy over-view?
BIRON.    Not you to me, but I betray'd by you:
    I, that am honest; I, that hold it sin
    To break the vow I am engaged in;
    I am betray'd, by keeping company
    With men like you, men of inconstancy.
    When shall you see me write a thing in rhyme?       180
    Or groan for love? or spend a minute's time
    In pruning me? When shall you hear that I
    Will praise a hand, a foot, a face, an eye,
    A gait, a state, a brow, a breast, a waist,
    A leg, a limb?—
KING.             Soft! whither away so fast?
    A true man or a thief that gallops so?
BIRON.    I post from love: good lover, let me go.

*Enter* JAQUENETTA *and* COSTARD

JAQ.    God bless the king!
KING.             What present hast thou there?       190
COST.    Some certain treason.
KING.             What makes treason here?
COST.    Nay, it makes nothing, sir.
KING.             If it mar nothing neither,
    The treason and you go in peace away together.
JAQ.    I beseech your Grace, let this letter be read:
    Our parson misdoubts it; 't was treason, he said.

---

164 *gnat*] used to convey the notion of insignificance.

KING. Biron, read it over.                                   [*Giving him the paper.*
         Where hadst thou it?
JAQ.      Of Costard.                                            200
KING.    Where hadst thou it?
COST.     Of Dun Adramadio, Dun Adramadio.
                                    [BIRON *tears the letter.*
KING.    How now! what is in you? why dost thou tear it?
BIRON.    A toy, my liege, a toy: your Grace needs not fear it.
LONG.    It did move him to passion, and therefore let's hear it.
DUM.    It is Biron's writing, and here is his name.
                                   [*Gathering up the pieces.*
BIRON. [*To* COSTARD]   Ah, you whoreson loggerhead! you were
         born to do me shame.
      Guilty, my lord, guilty! I confess, I confess.
KING.    What?
BIRON.    That you three fools lack'd me fool to make up the
         mess:                                           210
      He, he, and you, and you, my liege, and I,
      Are pick-purses in love, and we deserve to die.
      O, dismiss this audience, and I shall tell you more.
DUM.    Now the number is even.
BIRON.                               True, true; we are four.
      Will these turtles be gone?
KING.                          Hence, sirs; away!
COST.    Walk aside the true folk, and let the traitors stay.
                       [*Exeunt* COSTARD *and* JAQUENETTA.
BIRON.    Sweet lords, sweet lovers, O, let us embrace!
         As true we are as flesh and blood can be:             220
      The sea will ebb and flow, heaven show his face;
         Young blood doth not obey an old decree:
      We cannot cross the cause why we were born;
      Therefore of all hands must we be forsworn.
KING.    What, did these rent lines show some love of thine?
BIRON.    Did they, quoth you? Who sees the heavenly Rosaline,
      That, like a rude and savage man of Inde,
         At the first opening of the gorgeous east,

---

210 *to make up the mess*] to make up the company of four which constituted the num-
     ber of persons ordinarily dining at one table at the Inns of Court and at other for-
     mal convivial gatherings. Cf. *infra*, V, ii, 382.
219–224 *Sweet . . . forsworn*] Again Biron speaks in the six-line stanza of *Venus and
     Adonis*, as at I, i, 149–160, *supra*.

Bows not his vassal head and strucken blind
    Kisses the base ground with obedient breast?        230
What peremptory eagle-sighted eye
    Dares look upon the heaven of her brow,
That is not blinded by her majesty?
KING.    What zeal, what fury hath inspired thee now?
My love, her mistress, is a gracious moon;
    She an attending star, scarce seen a light.
BIRON.    My eyes are then no eyes, nor I Biron:
    O, but for my love, day would turn to night!
Of all complexions the cull'd sovereignty
    Do meet, as at a fair, in her fair cheek;        240
Where several worthies make one dignity,
    Where nothing wants that want itself doth seek.
Lend me the flourish of all gentle tongues, —
    Fie, painted rhetoric! O, she needs it not:
To things of sale a seller's praise belongs,
    She passes praise; then praise too short doth blot.
A wither'd hermit, five-score winters worn,
    Might shake off fifty, looking in her eye:
Beauty doth varnish age, as if new-born
    And gives the crutch the cradle's infancy:        250
O, 't is the sun that maketh all things shine.
KING.    By heaven, thy love is black as ebony.
BIRON.    Is ebony like her? O wood divine!
    A wife of such wood were felicity.
O, who can give an oath? where is a book?
    That I may swear beauty doth beauty lack,
If that she learn not of her eye to look:
    No face is fair that is not full so black.
KING.    O paradox! Black is the badge of hell,
    The hue of dungeons and the school of night;        260
And beauty's crest becomes the heavens well.
BIRON.    Devils soonest tempt, resembling spirits of light.
    O, if in black my lady's brows be deck'd,

---

229 *Bows . . . head*] This beautiful image from sun worship is also found in *Sonnet* vii,
    1–4:

> "Lo! in the orient when the gracious light
> Lifts up his burning head, each under eye
> Doth homage to his new-appearing sight,
> Serving with looks his sacred majesty."

258 *black*] The significance of a black complexion is a frequent theme of Renaissance
    poetry in western Europe. Shakespeare further develops it in his *Sonnets*, cxxvii and
    cxxxii.

It mourns that painting and usurping hair
Should ravish doters with a false aspect;
   And therefore is she born to make black fair.
Her favour turns the fashion of the days,
   For native blood is counted painting now;
And therefore red, that would avoid dispraise,
   Paints itself black, to imitate her brow.                    270

DUM.    To look like her are chimney-sweepers black.

LONG.   And since her time are colliers counted bright.

KING.   And Ethiopes of their sweet complexion crack.

DUM.    Dark needs no candles now, for dark is light.

BIRON.   Your mistresses dare never come in rain,
For fear their colours should be wash'd away.

KING.   'T were good, yours did; for, sir, to tell you plain,
I'll find a fairer face not wash'd to-day.

BIRON.   I'll prove her fair, or talk till doomsday here.

KING.   No devil will fright thee then so much as she.          280

DUM.    I never knew man hold vile stuff so dear.

LONG.   Look, here's thy love: my foot and her face see.

BIRON.   O, if the streets were paved with thine eyes,
Her feet were much too dainty for such tread!

DUM.    O vile! then, as she goes, what upward lies
The street should see as she walk'd overhead.

KING.   But what of this? are we not all in love?

BIRON.   Nothing so sure; and thereby all forsworn.

KING.   Then leave this chat; and, good Biron, now prove
Our loving lawful, and our faith not torn.                      290

DUM.    Ay, marry, there; some flattery for this evil.

LONG.   O, some authority how to proceed;
Some tricks, some quillets, how to cheat the devil.

DUM.    Some salve for perjury.

BIRON.                                        'T is more than need.
Have at you, then, affection's men at arms.
Consider what you first did swear unto,
To fast, to study, and to see no woman;
Flat treason 'gainst the kingly state of youth.
Say, can you fast? your stomachs are too young;                 300
And abstinence engenders maladies.

---

**264** *usurping hair*] Shakespeare makes numerous references to the wearing of false hair.

And where that you have vow'd to study, lords,
In that each of you have forsworn his book,
Can you still dream and pore and thereon look?
For when would you, my Lord, or you, or you,
Have found the ground of study's excellence
Without the beauty of a woman's face?
From women's eyes this doctrine I derive;
They are the ground, the books, the academes
From whence doth spring the true Promethean fire.          310
Why, universal plodding prisons up
The nimble spirits in the arteries,
As motion and long-during action tires
The sinewy vigour of the traveller.
Now, for not looking on a woman's face,
You have in that forsworn the use of eyes
And study too, the causer of your vow;
For where is any author in the world
Teaches such beauty as a woman's eye?
Learning is but an adjunct to ourself,                       320
And where we are our learning likewise is,
Then when ourselves we see in ladies' eyes,
Do we not likewise see our learning there?
O, we have made a vow to study, lords,
And in that vow we have forsworn our books.
For when would you, my liege, or you, or you,
In leaden contemplation have found out
Such fiery numbers as the prompting eyes
Of beauty's tutors have enrich'd you with?
Other slow arts entirely keep the brain;                     330
And therefore, finding barren practisers,
Scarce show a harvest of their heavy toil:
But love, first learned in a lady's eyes,
Lives not alone immured in the brain;
But, with the motion of all elements,
Courses as swift as thought in every power,

302–303 *And where that you . . . book*] This speech was clearly rewritten by Shakespeare
after he had first drafted it, and the printed text combines together many revised
and unrevised passages. The two lines quoted reappear with slight textual variations
in ll. 324–325, *infra*. It will be noticed that the three lines, 305–307 ("For when
would you . . . woman's face?") are similarly repeated in lines 326–329 ("For when
would you . . . with?"), while ll. 308–310 ("From women's eyes," etc.) are again repeated in ll. 356–359. In each case the lines which figure in the earlier part of
speech present the first or unrevised version. Cf. *infra*, V, ii, 839–844 and note.
311 *prisons*] Theobald's emendation of *poysons* in the original editions.

And gives to every power a double power,
Above their functions and their offices.
It adds a precious seeing to the eye;
A lover's eyes will gaze an eagle blind;　　　　　　　340
A lover's ear will hear the lowest sound,
When the suspicious head of theft is stopp'd:
Love's feeling is more soft and sensible
Than are the tender horns of cockled snails;
Love's tongue proves dainty Bacchus gross in taste:
For valour, is not Love a Hercules,
Still climbing trees in the Hesperides?
Subtle as Sphinx; as sweet and musical
As bright Apollo's lute, strung with his hair;
And when Love speaks, the voice of all the gods　　　350
Make heaven drowsy with the harmony.
Never durst poet touch a pen to write
Until his ink were temper'd with Love's sighs;
O, then his lines would ravish savage ears,
And plant in tyrants mild humility.
From women's eyes this doctrine I derive:
They sparkle still the right Promethean fire;
They are the books, the arts, the academes,
That show, contain and nourish all the world:
Else none at all in aught proves excellent.　　　　360
Then fools you were these women to forswear;
Or keeping what is sworn, you will prove fools.
For wisdom's sake, a word that all men love;
Or for love's sake, a word that loves all men;
Or for men's sake, the authors of these women;
Or women's sake, by whom we men are men;
Let us once lose our oaths to find ourselves,
Or else we lose ourselves to keep our oaths.
It is religion to be thus forsworn,

342 *the suspicious head of theft*] This seems equivalent to "the head suspicious of theft."
The general meaning is that the hearing of the lover is more alert and sharper than
that of the owner of treasure who lives in dread of thieves. Speed talks similarly of
watching "like one that fears robbing" (*Two Gent.*, II, i, 22).
347 *Hesperides*] In Greek mythology the nymphs, who guard the golden apples in the
isles of the blest, are known as the *Hesperides*, being daughters of Hesperus. Here
the name is applied to the islands themselves. The transference is common in
Elizabethan literature.
364 *loves all men*] "Loves" is explained by Capell as "is a friend to." Hanmer reads
*moves*, which suggests the requisite sense.

  For charity itself fulfils the law,                                    370
  And who can sever love from charity?
KING. Saint Cupid, then! and, soldiers, to the field!
BIRON. Advance your standards, and upon them, lords;
  Pell-mell, down with them! but be first advised,
  In conflict that you get the sun of them.
LONG. Now to plain-dealing; lay these glozes by:
  Shall we resolve to woo these girls of France?
KING. And win them too: therefore let us devise
  Some entertainment for them in their tents.
BIRON. First, from the park let us conduct them thither;        380
  Then homeward every man attach the hand
  Of his fair mistress: in the afternoon
  We will with some strange pastime solace them,
  Such as the shortness of the time can shape;
  For revels, dances, masks and merry hours
  Forerun fair Love, strewing her way with flowers.
KING. Away, away! no time shall be omitted
  That will betime, and may by us be fitted.
BIRON. Allons! allons! Sow'd cockle reap'd no corn;
  And justice always whirls in equal measure:                    390
  Light wenches may prove plagues to men forsworn;
  If so, our copper buys no better treasure.  *[Exeunt.*

---

375 *get the sun*] An allusion to the archer's anxiety to shoot with the sun at his back instead of in his face.
389 *Sow'd cockle*] A proverbial expression, implying here that the ladies will be won only if the preliminary measures be adequate.

# ACT V.

## SCENE I. *The Same.*

*Enter* HOLOFERNES, NATHANIEL, *and* DULL

HOLOFERNES.  Satis Quod Sufficit.

NATH.  I praise God for you, sir: your reasons at dinner have
been sharp and sententious; pleasant without scurrility, witty
without affection, audacious without impudency, learned
without opinion, and strange without heresy. I did converse
this quondam day with a companion of the king's, who is in-
tituled, nominated, or called, Don Adriano de Armado.

HOL.  Novi hominem tanquam te: his humour is lofty, his discourse peremptory, his tongue filed, his eye ambitious, his
gait majestical, and his general behaviour vain, ridiculous,         10
and thrasonical. He is too picked, too spruce, too affected,
too odd, as it were, too peregrinate, as I may call it.

NATH.  A most singular and choice epithet.
                                            [*Draws out his table-book.*

HOL.  He draweth out the thread of his verbosity finer than the
staple of his argument. I abhor such fanatical phantasimes,
such insociable and point-devise companions; such rackers
of orthography, as to speak dout, fine, when he should say
doubt; det, when he should pronounce debt,—d, e, b, t, not
d, e, t: he clepeth a calf, cauf; half hauf, neighbour vocatur
nebour; neigh abbreviated ne. This is abhominable,—which     20
he would call abbominable: it insinuateth me of insanie: ne
intelligis, domine? to make frantic, lunatic.

---

8 *Novi hominem tanquam te*] This phrase occurs in Lily's school grammar (1527), a
standard educational manual of the day.

20 *abhominable*] This was the common orthography in the sixteenth century, probably
from the mistaken notion that the word was derived from "ab homine" and not from
"ab omine." Holofernes champions the popular error.

NATH.  Laus Deo, bene intelligo.
HOL.  Bon, bon, fort bon! Priscian a little scratched; 't will serve.
NATH.  Videsne quis venit?
HOL.  Video, et gaudeo.

*Enter* ARMADO, MOTH, *and* COSTARD

ARM.  Chirrah!                                          [*To* MOTH.
HOL.  Quare chirrah, not sirrah?
ARM.  Men of peace, well encountered.
HOL.  Most military sir, salutation.                       30
MOTH.  [*Aside to* COSTARD]  They have been at a great feast of
    languages, and stolen the scraps.
COST.  O, they have lived long on the alms-basket of words. I
    marvel thy master hath not eaten thee for a word; for thou
    art not so long by the head as honorificabilitudinitatibus:
    thou art easier swallowed than a flap-dragon.
MOTH.  Peace! the peal begins.
ARM.  [*To* HOL.]  Monsieur, are you not lettered?
MOTH.  Yes, yes; he teaches boys the horn-book.
    What is a, b, spelt backward, with the horn on his head?    40
HOL.  Ba, pueritia, with a horn added.
MOTH.  Ba, most silly sheep with a horn. You hear his learning.
HOL.  Quis, quis, thou consonant?
MOTH.  The third of the five vowels, if you repeat them; or the
    fifth, if I.
HOL.  I will repeat them,—a, e, i,—
MOTH.  The sheep: the other two concludes it,—o, u.
ARM.  Now, by the salt wave of the Mediterraneum, a sweet
    touch, a quick venue of wit,—snip, snap, quick and home! it
    rejoiceth my intellect: true wit!                        50
MOTH.  Offered by a child to an old man; which is wit-old.
HOL.  What is the figure? what is the figure?

24 *Priscian a little scratched*] These Latin phrases are derived from conversation books
    frequently used in Elizabethan schools. Cf. *Familiares colloquendi formulae in usum
    scholarum concinnatae*: "He speaks false Latin, diminuit Prisciani caput. 'Tis bar-
    barous Latin, olet barbariem." The last phrase suggested "I smell false Latin," V, i,
    64, *infra*.
35 *honorificabilitudinitatibus*] This long word, which is frequently met with in medieval
    Latin, is cited by Dante in his *De vulgari eloquentia* (1300?) as a word difficult to em-
    ploy in poetry. Elizabethan writers often employ it derisively. Cf. Nashe's *Lenten
    Stuffe*, 1599 (Nashe's Works, ed. McKerrow, Vol. III, p. 176).
49 *venue*] a thrust in fencing. In Ben Jonson's *Every Man in his Humour*, Act I, Sc. iv,
    Bobadill uses the word as synonymous with "stoccata," a more technical term for the
    fencer's thrust or lunge.

MOTH.   Horns.

HOL.    Thou disputest like an infant: go, whip thy gig.

MOTH.   Lend me your horn to make one, and I will whip about
        your infamy circum circa,—a gig of a cuckold's horn.

COST.   An I had but one penny in the world, thou shouldst have
        it to buy gingerbread: hold, there is the very remuneration I
        had of thy master, thou halfpenny purse of wit, thou pigeon-
        egg of discretion. O, an the heavens were so pleased that        60
        thou wert but my bastard, what a joyful father wouldst thou
        make me! Go to; thou hast it ad dunghill, at the fingers'
        ends, as they say.

HOL.    O, I smell false Latin; dunghill for unguem.

ARM.    Arts-man, preambulate, we will be singuled from the bar-
        barous. Do you not educate youth at the charge-house on
        the top of the mountain?

HOL.    Or mons, the hill.

ARM.    At your sweet pleasure, for the mountain.

HOL.    I do, sans question.                                              70

ARM.    Sir, it is the king's most sweet pleasure and affection to
        congratulate the princess at her pavilion in the posteriors of
        this day, which the rude multitude call the afternoon.

HOL.    The posterior of the day, most generous sir, is liable, con-
        gruent and measurable for the afternoon: the word is well
        culled, chose, sweet and apt, I do assure you, sir, I do assure.

ARM.    Sir, the king is a noble gentleman, and my familiar, I do
        assure ye, very good friend: for what is inward between us, let
        it pass. I do beseech thee, remember thy courtesy; I beseech
        thee, apparel thy head: and among other important and         80
        most serious designs, and of great import indeed, too, but let
        that pass: for I must tell thee, it will please his Grace, by the
        world, sometime to lean upon my poor shoulder, and with
        his royal finger, thus, dally with my excrement, with my
        mustachio; but, sweet heart, let that pass. By the world, I

---

64 *I smell false Latin*] See note on V, i, 24, *supra*.

   *ad unguem*] Another phrase from Lily's Grammar. Cf. l. 8, *supra*. It is classical Latin,
   and means "to the nail," "polished." Cf. Hor. Sat. l. 5. 31–32, "*ad unguem* factus
   homo."

66 *charge-house*] Affected periphrasis for a "school" where the *charge* of youth is under-
   taken.

79 *remember thy courtesy*] Holofernes having removed his hat is bidden by Armado replace it. He reminds the pedant that to replace one's hat on one's head after raising
   it satisfies all requirements of courtesy. Cf. Ben Jonson, *Every Man in his Humour*,
   I, ii, 49–51: *Knowell* (to servant). "Pray you *remember your courtesy* . . . nay, *pray be
   covered*."

recount no fable; some certain special honours it pleaseth
his greatness to impart to Armado, a soldier, a man of travel,
that hath seen the world; but let that pass. The very all of all
is,—but, sweet heart, I do implore secrecy,—that the king
would have me present the princess, sweet chuck, with some          90
delightful ostentation, or show, or pageant, or antique, or
firework. Now, understanding that the curate and your sweet
self are good at such eruptions and sudden breaking out of
mirth, as it were, I have acquainted you withal, to the end to
crave your assistance.

HOL.  Sir, you shall present before her the Nine Worthies. Sir,
as concerning some entertainment of time, some show in
the posterior of this day, to be rendered by our assistants, at
the king's command, and this most gallant, illustrate, and
learned gentleman, before the princess; I say none so fit as          100
to present the Nine Worthies.

NATH.  Where will you find men worthy enough to present
them?

HOL.  Joshua, yourself; myself and this gallant gentleman, Judas
Maccabæus; this swain, because of his great limb or joint,
shall pass Pompey the Great; the page, Hercules,—

ARM.  Pardon, sir; error: he is not quantity enough for that
Worthy's thumb: he is not so big as the end of his club.

HOL.  Shall I have audience? he shall present Hercules in mi-
nority: his enter and exit shall be strangling a snake; and I          110
will have an apology for that purpose.

MOTH.  An excellent device! so, if any of the audience hiss, you
may cry, "Well done, Hercules! now thou crushest the
snake!" that is the way to make an offence gracious, though
few have the grace to do it.

ARM.  For the rest of the Worthies?—

HOL.  I will play three myself.

MOTH.  Thrice-worthy gentleman!

ARM.  Shall I tell you a thing?

HOL.  We attend.                                                       120

ARM.  We will have, if this fadge not, an antique. I beseech you,
follow.

96 *Nine Worthies*] According to the tradition of medieval literature, these were three pa-
gans, Hector, Alexander, and Julius Cæsar; three Jews, Joshua, David, and Judas
Maccabæus; three Christians, Arthur, Charlemagne, and Godfrey of Bouillon. The
show actually presented *infra*, at V, ii, 566 *seq.*, includes no more than five worthies,
of which three alone belong to the traditional list, namely, Alexander, Judas
Maccabæus, and Hector. The other two, Pompey and Hercules, who there accom-
pany them, are without literary authority.

HOL.   Via, goodman Dull! thou hast spoken no word all this
    while.
DULL.   Nor understood none neither, sir.
HOL.   Allons! we will employ thee.
DULL.   I'll make one in a dance, or so; or I will play
    On the tabor to the Worthies, and let them dance the hay.
HOL.   Most dull, honest Dull! To our sport away!          [*Exeunt.*

## SCENE II. *The Same.*

*Enter the* PRINCESS, KATHARINE, ROSALINE *and* MARIA

PRIN.   Sweet hearts, we shall be rich ere we depart,
    If fairings come thus plentifully in:
    A lady wall'd about with diamonds!
    Look you what I have from the loving king.
ROS.   Madam, came nothing else along with that?
PRIN.   Nothing but this! yes, as much love in rhyme
    As would be cramm'd up in a sheet of paper,
    Writ o' both sides the leaf, margent and all,
    That he was fain to seal on Cupid's name.
ROS.   That was the way to make his godhead wax,          10
    For he hath been five thousand years a boy.
KATH.   Ay, and a shrewd unhappy gallows too.
ROS.   You'll ne'er be friends with him; a' kill'd your sister.
KATH.   He made her melancholy, sad, and heavy;
    And so she died: had she been light, like you,
    Of such a merry, nimble, stirring spirit,
    She might ha' been a grandam ere she died:
    And so may you; for a light heart lives long.
ROS.   What's your dark meaning, mouse, of this light word?
KATH.   A light condition in a beauty dark.          20
ROS.   We need more light to find your meaning out.
KATH.   You'll mar the light by taking it in snuff;
    Therefore I'll darkly end the argument.

---

12 *gallows*] In Sidney's *Arcadia*, Bk. I, c. 16, p. 165 (1590), Cupid is called a hangman,
   *i.e.* executioner. Here "gallows" seems used in the same sense. But it has also been
   interpreted "gallowsbird," which has contemporary authority, and also as "mischie-
   vous imp," which is not uncommon in provincial dialect use.

15 *light*] In the quibbles which follow, this word is employed in the varied senses of
   *without weight, luminous, nimble, frivolous, wanton, merry.*

22 *taking it in snuff*] The verbal play is on the two meanings of the word "snuff,"
   namely: "candle-ash" and "anger."

ROS.    Look, what you do, you do it still i' th' dark.
KATH.    So do not you, for you are a light wench.
ROS.    Indeed, I weigh not you, and therefore light.
KATH.    You weigh me not?—O, that's you care not for me.
ROS.    Great reason; for "past cure is still past care."
PRIN.    Well bandied both; a set of wit well play'd.
      But, Rosaline, you have a favour too:      30
      Who sent it? and what is it?
ROS.                    I would you knew:
      And if my face were but as fair as yours,
      My favour were as great; be witness this.
      Nay, I have verses too, I thank Biron:
      The numbers true; and, were the numbering too,
      I were the fairest goddess on the ground:
      I am compared to twenty thousand fairs.
      O, he hath drawn my picture in his letter!
PRIN.    Any thing like?      40
ROS.    Much in the letters; nothing in the praise.
PRIN.    Beauteous as ink; a good conclusion.
KATH.    Fair as a text B in a copy-book.
ROS.    'Ware pencils, ho! let me not die your debtor,
      My red dominical, my golden letter:
      O that your face were not so full of O's!
KATH.    A pox of that jest! and I beshrew all shrows.
PRIN.    But, Katharine, what was sent to you from fair Dumain?
KATH.    Madam, this glove.
PRIN.               Did he not send you twain?      50
KATH.    Yes, madam, and, moreover,
      Some thousand verses of a faithful lover,
      A huge translation of hypocrisy,
      Vilely compiled, profound simplicity.
MAR.    This and these pearls to me sent Longaville:
      The letter is too long by half a mile.
PRIN.    I think no less. Dost thou not wish in heart
      The chain were longer and the letter short?
MAR.    Ay, or I would these hands might never part.
PRIN.    We are wise girls to mock our lovers so.      60
ROS.    They are worse fools to purchase mocking so.
      That same Biron I'll torture ere I go:

29 *bandied . . . set*] terms used in tennis.
45 *red . . . letter*] The "dominical" letter used to denote Sundays in old almanacs was printed in red, which was reckoned the colour of gold.
46 *O's*] pockmarks.

          O that I knew he were but in by the week!
          How I would make him fawn, and beg, and seek,
          And wait the season, and observe the times.
          And spend his prodigal wits in bootless rhymes,
          And shape his service wholly to my hests,
          And make him proud to make me proud that jests!
          So perttaunt-like would I o'ersway his state,
          That he should be my fool, and I his fate.                      70
PRIN.   None are so surely caught, when they are catch'd,
          As wit turn'd fool: folly, in wisdom hatch'd,
          Hath wisdom's warrant and the help of school,
          And wit's own grace to grace a learned fool.
ROS.    The blood of youth burns not with such excess
          As gravity's revolt to wantonness.
MAR.    Folly in fools bears not so strong a note
          As foolery in the wise, when wit doth dote;
          Since all the power thereof it doth apply
          To prove, by wit, worth in simplicity.                         80
PRIN.   Here comes Boyet, and mirth is in his face.

*Enter* BOYET

BOYET.   O, I am stabb'd with laughter! Where's her Grace?
PRIN.   Thy news, Boyet?
BOYET.                    Prepare, madam, prepare!
          Arm, wenches, arm! encounters mounted are
          Against your peace: Love doth approach disguised,
          Armed in arguments; you'll be surprised:
          Muster your wits; stand in your own defence;
          Or hide your heads like cowards, and fly hence.
PRIN.   Saint Denis to Saint Cupid! What are they                      90
          That charge their breath against us? say, scout, say.
BOYET.   Under the cool shade of a sycamore
          I thought to close mine eyes some half an hour;
          When, lo! to interrupt my purposed rest,
          Toward that shade I might behold addrest
          The king and his companions: warily
          I stole into a neighbour thicket by,

63 *in by the week*] hired by the week, in servitude or bondage, enslaved.
69 *perttaunt-like*] This reading of the early editions is puzzling. The most popular emen-
     dations are *portent-like* and *potent-like, i.e.* tyrant-like or tyrannically. But neither is
     satisfactory. There was a verb "pert," "to behave *pertly*, briskly, resolutely"; and it is
     possible that Shakespeare may have formed from it the adverb "perting-like," *i.e.* per-
     tingly, pertly, briskly. Biron is called "pert" (in the different sense of "saucy") at 290,
     *infra*.

And overheard what you shall overhear;
That, by and by, disguised they will be here.
Their herald is a pretty knavish page,                    100
That well by heart hath conn'd his embassage:
Action and accent did they teach him there;
"Thus must thou speak," and "thus thy body bear:"
And ever and anon they made a doubt
Presence majestical would put him out;
"For," quoth the king, "an angel shalt thou see;
Yet fear not thou, but speak audaciously."
The boy replied, "An angel is not evil;
I should have fear'd her, had she been a devil."
With that, all laugh'd, and clapped him on the shoulder,   110
Making the bold wag by their praises bolder:
One rubb'd his elbow thus, and fleer'd and swore
A better speech was never spoke before;
Another, with his finger and his thumb,
Cried, "Via! we will do 't, come what will come;"
The third he caper'd, and cried, "All goes well;"
The fourth turn'd on the toe, and down he fell.
With that, they all did tumble on the ground,
With such a zealous laughter, so profound,
That in this spleen ridiculous appears,                    120
To check their folly, passion's solemn tears.
PRIN.    But what, but what, come they to visit us?
BOYET.    They do, they do; and are apparell'd thus,
Like Muscovites or Russians, as I guess.
Their purpose is to parle, to court and dance;
And every one his love-feat will advance
Unto his several mistress, which they'll know
By favours several which they did bestow.
PRIN.    And will they so? the gallants shall be task'd;
For, ladies, we will every one be mask'd;                  130
And not a man of them shall have the grace,
Despite of suit, to see a lady's face.
Hold, Rosaline, this favour thou shalt wear,
And then the king will court thee for his dear;

124 *Muscovites or Russians*] The chronicler Hall relates how, at a royal banquet in the first year of Henry VIII (1510), two English courtiers came fancifully arrayed in barbaric richness "after the fashion of Russia or Russland." But in all probability Shakespeare had in mind the more recent appearance of ambassadors from Russia at Queen Elizabeth's court with a view to selecting from Englishwomen a wife for the Tsar.

      Hold, take thou this, my sweet, and give me thine,
      So shall Biron take me for Rosaline.
      And change you favours too; so shall your loves
      Woo contrary, deceived by these removes.
ROS.   Come on, then; wear the favours most in sight.
KATH.   But in this changing what is your intent?        140
PRIN.   The effect of my intent is to cross theirs:
      They do it but in mocking merriment;
      And mock for mock is only my intent.
      Their several counsels they unbosom shall
      To loves mistook, and so be mock'd withal
      Upon the next occasion that we meet,
      With visages display'd, to talk and greet.
ROS.   But shall we dance, if they desire us to 't?
PRIN.   No, to the death, we will not move a foot:
      Nor to their penn'd speech render we no grace;      150
      But while 't is spoke each turn away her face.
BOYET.   Why, that contempt will kill the speaker's heart,
      And quite divorce his memory from his part.
PRIN.   Therefore I do it; and I make no doubt
      The rest will ne'er come in, if he be out.
      There's no such sport as sport by sport o'erthrown;
      To make theirs ours, and ours none but our own:
      So shall we stay, mocking intended game,
      And they, well mock'd, depart away with shame.
                        *[Trumpets sound within.*
BOYET.   The trumpet sounds: be mask'd; the maskers come.   160
                           *[The Ladies mask.*

*Enter Blackmoors with music;* MOTH; *the* KING, BIRON,
LONGAVILLE, *and* DUMAIN, *in Russian habits, and masked*

MOTH.   All hail, the richest beauties on the earth!—
BOYET.   Beauties no richer than rich taffeta.
MOTH.   A holy parcel of the fairest dames
                *[The Ladies turn their backs to him.*
      That ever turn'd their—backs—to mortal views!
BIRON. *[Aside to* MOTH]   Their eyes, villain, their eyes.
MOTH.   That ever turn'd their eyes to mortal views!—
      Out—
BOYET.   True; out indeed.
MOTH.   Out of your favours, heavenly spirits, vouchsafe
      Not to behold—                            170

162 *rich taffeta*] The masks of the ladies were of rich taffeta silk.

BIRON. [*Aside to* MOTH]   Once to behold, rogue.
MOTH.   Once to behold with your sun-beamed eyes,
——with your sun-beamed eyes—
BOYET.   They will not answer to that epithet;
You were best call it "daughter-beamed eyes."
MOTH.   They do not mark me, and that brings me out.
BIRON.   Is this your perfectness? be gone, you rogue!

                                  [*Exit* MOTH.

ROS.   What would these strangers? know their minds, Boyet:
If they do speak our language, 't is our will
That some plain man recount their purposes:            180
Know what they would.
BOYET.   What would you with the princess?
BIRON.   Nothing but peace and gentle visitation.
ROS.   What would they, say they?
BOYET.   Nothing but peace and gentle visitation.
ROS.   Why, that they have; and bid them so be gone.
BOYET.   She says, you have it, and you may be gone.
KING.   Say to her, we have measured many miles
To tread a measure with her on this grass.
BOYET.   They say, that they have measured many a mile            190
To tread a measure with you on this grass.
ROS.   It is not so. Ask them how many inches
Is in one mile: if they have measured many,
The measure then of one is easily told.
BOYET.   If to come hither you have measured miles,
And many miles, the princess bids you tell
How many inches doth fill up one mile.
BIRON.   Tell her, we measure them by weary steps.
BOYET.   She hears herself.
ROS.                          How many weary steps,            200
Of many weary miles you have o'ergone,
Are number'd in the travel of one mile?
BIRON.   We number nothing that we spend for you:
Our duty is so rich, so infinite,
That we may do it still without accompt.
Vouchsafe to show the sunshine of your face,
That we, like savages, may worship it.
ROS.   My face is but a moon, and clouded too.
KING.   Blessed are clouds, to do as such clouds do!
Vouchsafe, bright moon, and these thy stars, to shine,            210
Those clouds removed, upon our watery eyne.
ROS.   O vain petitioner! beg a greater matter;

Thou now request'st but moonshine in the water.
KING.    Then, in our measure do but vouchsafe one change.
Thou bid'st me beg: this begging is not strange.
ROS.    Play, music, then! Nay, you must do it soon.
                                                    [*Music plays.*
Not yet! no dance! Thus change I like the moon.
KING.    Will you not dance? How come you thus estranged?
ROS.    You took the moon at full, but now she's changed.
KING.    Yet still she is the moon, and I the man.              220
The music plays; vouchsafe some motion to it.
ROS.    Our ears vouchsafe it.
KING.                          But your legs should do it.
ROS.    Since you are strangers, and come here by chance,
We'll not be nice: take hands. We will not dance.
KING.    Why take we hands, then?
ROS.                              Only to part friends:
Curtsey, sweet hearts; and so the measure ends.
KING.    More measure of this measure; be not nice.
ROS.    We can afford no more at such a price.                  230
KING.    Prize you yourselves: what buys your company?
ROS.    Your absence only.
KING.                      That can never be.
ROS.    Then cannot we be bought: and so, adieu;
Twice to your visor, and half once to you.
KING.    If you deny to dance, let's hold more chat.
ROS.    In private, then.
KING.                      I am best pleased with that.
                                              [*They converse apart.*
BIRON.    White-handed mistress, one sweet word with thee.
PRIN.    Honey, and milk, and sugar; there is three.           240
BIRON.    Nay then, two treys, an if you grow so nice,
Metheglin, wort, and malmsey: well run, dice!
There's half-a-dozen sweets.
PRIN.                          Seventh sweet, adieu:
Since you can cog, I'll play no more with you.

235 *Twice to your visor*] She bids a double adieu to his disguise, not wishing to see it
    again; but only half a farewell to himself, as she has no wish of making the parting
    permanent.
241 *treys*] throws of threes at dice.
242 *Metheglin, wort, and malmsey*] three sweet liquors: metheglin was made from
    honey; wort was unfermented beer; malmsey a sweet wine originally made in
    Greece, which Chaucer knew as *malvesie* from the French *malvoisie;* cf. Italian
    *malvasia.* The word is said to be formed from the name of the modern Greek
    city Monembasía, a Laconian seaport.

BIRON.    One word in secret.
PRIN.                            Let it not be sweet.
BIRON.    Thou grievest my gall.
PRIN.                                Gall! bitter.
BIRON.                                          Therefore meet.    250
                            [*They converse apart.*

DUM.    Will you vouchsafe with me to change a word?
MAR.    Name it.
DUM.                Fair lady,—
MAR.                        Say you so? Fair lord,—
    Take that for your fair lady.
DUM.                            Please it you,
    As much in private, and I'll bid adieu.
                            [*They converse apart.*

KATH.    What, was your vizard made without a tongue?
LONG.    I know the reason, lady, why you ask.
KATH.    O for your reason! quickly, sir; I long.    260
LONG.    You have a double tongue within your mask,
    And would afford my speechless vizard half.
KATH.    Veal, quoth the Dutchman. Is not "veal" a calf?
LONG.    A calf, fair lady!
KATH.                    No, a fair lord calf.
LONG.    Let's part the word.
KATH.                    No, I'll not be your half:
    Take all, and wean it; it may prove an ox.
LONG.    Look, how you butt yourself in these sharp mocks!
    Will you give horns, chaste lady? do not so.    270
KATH.    Then die a calf, before your horns do grow.
LONG.    One word in private with you, ere I die.
KATH.    Bleat softly, then; the butcher hears you cry.
                            [*They converse apart.*

BOYET.    The tongues of mocking wenches are as keen
        As is the razor's edge invisible,
    Cutting a smaller hair than may be seen;
        Above the sense of sense; so sensible
    Seemeth their conference; their conceits have wings
    Fleeter than arrows, bullets, wind, thought, swifter things.
ROS.    Not one word more, my maids; break off, break off.    280

---

263 *Veal, quoth the Dutchman*] A joke on the common mispronunciation by Germans
    of "veal" or "vell" for "well." In the *Wisdom of Doctor Doddypoll*, 1600, a German
    doctor, who uses the word "veale," which he corrects to "vell," is said by his inter-
    locutor to "make a calf of" him.

BIRON.    By heaven, all dry-beaten with pure scoff!
KING.    Farewell, mad wenches; you have simple wits.
PRIN.    Twenty adieus, my frozen Muscovits.
                    [*Exeunt* KING, *Lords, and Blackamoors.*
        Are these the breed of wits so wonder'd at?
BOYET.    Tapers they are, with your sweet breaths puff'd out.
ROS.    Well-liking wits they have; gross, gross; fat, fat.
PRIN.    O poverty in wit, kingly-poor flout!
        Will they not, think you, hang themselves to-night?
        Or ever, but in vizards, show their faces?
        This pert Biron was out of countenance quite.                    290
ROS.    O, they were all in lamentable cases!
        The king was weeping-ripe for a good word.
PRIN.    Biron did swear himself out of all suit.
MAR.    Dumain was at my service, and his sword:
        No point, quoth I; my servant straight was mute.
KATH.    Lord Longaville said, I came o'er his heart;
        And trow you what he call'd me?
PRIN.                                    Qualm, perhaps.
KATH.    Yes, in good faith.
PRIN.                        Go, sickness as thou art!                    300
ROS.    Well, better wits have worn plain statute-caps.
        But will you hear? the king is my love sworn.
PRIN.    And quick Biron hath plighted faith to me.
KATH.    And Longaville was for my service born.
MAR.    Dumain is mine, as sure as bark on tree.
BOYET.    Madam, and pretty mistresses, give ear:
        Immediately they will again be here
        In their own shapes; for it can never be
        They will digest this harsh indignity.
PRIN.    Will they return?                                    310
BOYET.                        They will, they will, God knows,
        And leap for joy, though they are lame with blows:
        Therefore change favours; and, when they repair,
        Blow like sweet roses in this summer air.
PRIN.    How blow? how blow? speak to be understood.
BOYET.    Fair ladies mask'd are roses in their bud;

---

281 *dry-beaten*] beaten with blows which bruise but do not draw blood.
301 *statute-caps*] By Statute 13 Eliz. 1571 all, except persons of high rank, were bound
    to wear, on Sundays and holidays, thick woollen caps made in England. The text
    means that better wits may be found among the humbler class of citizens.

Dismask'd, their damask sweet commixture shown,
Are angels vailing clouds, or roses blown.
PRIN.   Avaunt, perplexity! What shall we do,
If they return in their own shapes to woo?                          320
ROS.   Good madam, if by me you'll be advised,
Let's mock them still, as well known as disguised:
Let us complain to them what fools were here,
Disguised like Muscovites, in shapeless gear;
And wonder what they were and to what end
Their shallow shows and prologue vilely penn'd,
And their rough carriage so ridiculous,
Should be presented at our tent to us.
BOYET.   Ladies, withdraw: the gallants are at hand.
PRIN.   Whip to our tents, as roes run o'er land.                   330
      [*Exeunt* PRINCESS, ROSALINE, KATHARINE, *and* MARIA.

*Re-enter the* KING, BIRON, LONGAVILLE, *and* DUMAIN, *in their*
      *proper habits.*

KING.   Fair sir, God save you! Where's the princess?
BOYET.   Gone to her tent. Please it your Majesty
Command me any service to her thither?
KING.   That she vouchsafe me audience for one word.
BOYET.   I will; and so will she, I know, my lord.        [*Exit.*
BIRON.   This fellow pecks up wit as pigeons pease,
And utters it again when God doth please:
He is wit's pedler, and retails his wares
At wakes and wassails, meetings, markets, fairs;
And we that sell by gross, the Lord doth know,                      340
Have not the grace to grace it with such show.
This gallant pins the wenches on his sleeve;
Had he been Adam, he had tempted Eve;
A' can carve too, and lisp: why, this is he
That kiss'd his hand away in courtesy;
This is the ape of form, monsieur the nice,
That, when he plays at tables, chides the dice
In honourable terms: nay, he can sing

---

317–318 *damask . . . blown*] The display of the "damasked" (*i.e.* variegated) mingling of
   red and white in the ladies' features is compared to the appearance of angels when
   clouds fall from before them, or to that of roses in full bloom. "Vail" means let fall,
   lower.
344 *carve*] The word is constantly used of unctuously complimentary phrases or ges-
   tures, and is commonly associated with the fantastically elaborate method of carv-
   ing meat for guests at table by way of showing hospitality.

A mean most meanly; and in ushering,
Mend him who can: the ladies call him sweet;                   350
The stairs, as he treads on them, kiss his feet:
This is the flower that smiles on every one,
To show his teeth as white as whale's bone;
And consciences, that will not die in debt,
Pay him the due of honey-tongued Boyet.

KING.   A blister on his sweet tongue, with my heart,
That put Armado's page out of his part!

BIRON.   See where it comes! Behaviour, what wert thou
Till this madman show'd thee? and what art thou now?

*Re-enter the* PRINCESS, *ushered by* BOYET; ROSALINE, MARIA, *and*
KATHARINE.

KING.   All hail, sweet madam, and fair time of day!            360
PRIN.   "Fair" in "all hail" is foul, as I conceive.
KING.   Construe my speeches better, if you may.
PRIN.   Then wish me better; I will give you leave.
KING.   We came to visit you, and purpose now
To lead you to our court; vouchsafe it then.
PRIN.   This field shall hold me; and so hold your vow:
Nor God, nor I, delights in perjured men.
KING.   Rebuke me not for that which you provoke:
The virtue of your eye must break my oath.
PRIN.   You nickname virtue; vice you should have spoke;         370
For virtue's office never breaks men's troth.
Now by my maiden honour yet as pure
As the unsullied lily I protest,
A world of torments though I should endure,
I would not yield to be your house's guest;
So much I hate a breaking cause to be
Of heavenly oaths, vow'd with integrity.
KING.   O, you have lived in desolation here,
Unseen, unvisited, much to our shame.
PRIN.   Not so, my lord; it is not so, I swear;                 380
We have had pastimes here and pleasant game:
A mess of Russians left us but of late.
KING.   How, madam! Russians!

---

361 *"Fair" in "all hail"*] The quibble on "hail" (*i.e.,* storm of hail) reappears in *Two
Noble Kinsmen,* III, v; Beaumont and Fletcher's *Faithful Friends,* III, ii; and
Dekker's *Old Fortunatus,* ed. Pearson, p. 113.
382 *mess*] See note on IV, iii, 210, *supra.*

PRIN.                              Ay, in truth, my lord;
    Trim gallants, full of courtship and of state.
ROS.    Madam, speak true. It is not so, my lord:
    My lady, to the manner of the days,
    In courtesy gives undeserving praise.
    We four indeed confronted were with four
    In Russian habit: here, they stay'd an hour,    390
    And talk'd apace; and in that hour, my lord,
    They did not bless us with one happy word.
    I dare not call them fools; but this I think,
    When they are thirsty, fools would fain have drink.
BIRON.    This jest is dry to me. Fair gentle sweet,
    Your wit makes wise things foolish: when we greet,
    With eyes best seeing, heaven's fiery eye,
    By light we lose light: your capacity
    Is of that nature that to your huge store
    Wise things seem foolish and rich things but poor.    400
ROS.    This proves you wise and rich, for in my eye,—
BIRON.    I am a fool, and full of poverty.
ROS.    But that you take what doth to you belong,
    It were a fault to snatch words from my tongue.
BIRON.    O, I am yours, and all that I possess!
ROS.    All the fool mine?
BIRON.            I cannot give you less.
ROS.    Which of the vizards was it that you wore?
BIRON.    Where? when? what vizard? why demand you this?
ROS.    There, then, that vizard; that superfluous case    410
    That hid the worse, and show'd the better face.
KING.    We are descried; they'll mock us now downright.
DUM.    Let us confess, and turn it to a jest.
PRIN.    Amazed, my lord? why looks your highness sad?
ROS.    Help, hold his brows! he'll swound! Why look you pale?
    Sea-sick, I think, coming from Muscovy.
BIRON.    Thus pour the stars down plagues for perjury.
    Can any face of brass hold longer out?
    Here stand I: lady, dart thy skill at me;
    Bruise me with scorn, confound me with a flout;    420
    Thrust thy sharp wit quite through my ignorance;
    Cut me to pieces with thy keen conceit;
    And I will wish thee never more to dance,
    Nor never more in Russian habit wait.
    O, never will I trust to speeches penn'd,
    Nor to the motion of a schoolboy's tongue;

Nor never come in vizard to my friend;
  Nor woo in rhyme, like a blind harper's song!
Taffeta phrases, silken terms precise,
  Three-piled hyperboles, spruce affectation,                    430
Figures pedantical; these summer-flies
  Have blown me full of maggot ostentation:
I do forswear them; and I here protest,
  By this white glove,—how white the hand, God knows!—
Henceforth my wooing mind shall be express'd
  In russet yeas, and honest kersey noes:
And, to begin, wench,—so God help me, la!—
My love to thee is sound, sans crack or flaw.
ROS.  Sans sans, I pray you.
BIRON.                          Yet I have a trick                 440
  Of the old rage:—bear with me, I am sick;
I'll leave it by degrees. Soft, let us see:
Write, "Lord have mercy on us" on those three;
They are infected; in their hearts it lies;
They have the plague, and caught it of your eyes;
These lords are visited; you are not free,
For the Lord's tokens on you do I see.
PRIN.  No, they are free that gave these tokens to us.
BIRON.  Our states are forfeit: seek not to undo us.
ROS.  It is not so; for how can this be true,                     450
  That you stand forfeit, being those that sue?
BIRON.  Peace! for I will not have to do with you.
ROS.  Nor shall not, if I do as I intend.
BIRON.  Speak for yourselves; my wit is at an end.
KING.  Teach us, sweet madam, for our rude transgression
  Some fair excuse.
PRIN.                    The fairest is confession.
  Were not you here but even now disguised?
KING.  Madam, I was.
PRIN.                   And were you well advised;               460
KING.  I was, fair madam.
PRIN.                       When you then were here,
  What did you whisper in your lady's ear?

432 *blown*] Used as in "fly blown" of infected meat.
439 *Sans sans*] Without sans, *i.e.* avoid French phrases.
443 *"Lord have mercy on us"*] These words were placarded on houses of which inmates
  were stricken by the plague.
447 *Lord's tokens*] plague spots. There is a pun here on the gifts given by the lords
  to the ladies.

KING.    That more than all the world I did respect her.

PRIN.    When she shall challenge this, you will reject her.

KING.    Upon mine honour, no.

PRIN.                                Peace, peace! forbear:
    Your oath once broke, you force not to forswear.

KING.    Despise me, when I break this oath of mine.

PRIN.    I will: and therefore keep it. Rosaline,                        470
    What did the Russian whisper in your ear?

ROS.    Madam, he swore that he did hold me dear
    As precious eyesight, and did value me
    Above this world; adding thereto, moreover,
    That he would wed me, or else die my lover.

PRIN.    God give thee joy of him! the noble lord
    Most honourably doth uphold his word.

KING.    What mean you, madam? by my life, my troth,
    I never swore this lady such an oath.

ROS.    By heaven, you did; and to confirm it plain,                    480
    You gave me this: but take it, sir, again.

KING.    My faith and this the princess I did give:
    I knew her by this jewel on her sleeve.

PRIN.    Pardon me, sir, this jewel did she wear;
    And Lord Biron, I thank him, is my dear.
    What, will you have me, or your pearl again?

BIRON.    Neither of either; I remit both twain.
    I see the trick on't: here was a consent,
    Knowing aforehand of our merriment,
    To dash it like a Christmas comedy:                              490
    Some carry-tale, some please-man, some slight zany,
    Some mumble-news, some trencher-knight, some Dick,
    That smiles his cheek in years, and knows the trick
    To make my lady laugh when she's disposed,
    Told our intents before; which once disclosed,
    The ladies did change favours; and then we,
    Following the signs, woo'd but the sign of she.
    Now, to our perjury to add more terror,
    We are again forsworn, in will and error.
    Much upon this it is: and might not you          [*To* BOYET.    500
    Forestall our sport, to make us thus untrue?

---

468 *force not*] do not mind or hesitate, make no matter.

493 *in years*] into years, old age. Laughter was commonly said to bring on wrinkles pre-
    maturely.

494 *disposed*] *sc.* to merriment. See note *supra*, II, i, 257.

496 *change favours*] exchange masks.

Do not you know my lady's foot by the squier,
  And laugh upon the apple of her eye?
And stand between her back, sir, and the fire,
  Holding a trencher, jesting merrily?
You put our page out: go, you are allow'd;
Die when you will, a smock shall be your shroud.
You leer upon me, do you? there's an eye
Wounds like a leaden sword.

BOYET.                          Full merrily          510
  Hath this brave manage, this career, been run.

BIRON.   Lo, he is tilting straight! Peace! I have done.

*Enter* COSTARD

  Welcome, pure wit! thou part'st a fair fray.

COST.   O Lord, sir, they would know
  Whether the three Worthies shall come in or no.

BIRON.   What, are there but three?

COST.                          No, sir; but it is vara fine,
  For every one pursents three.

BIRON.                          And three times thrice is nine.

COST.   Not so, sir; under correction, sir; I hope it is not so.          520
  You cannot beg us, sir, I can assure you, sir; we know what
    we know:
  I hope, sir, three times thrice, sir, —

BIRON.   Is not nine.

COST.   Under correction, sir, we know whereuntil it doth
  amount.

BIRON.   By Jove, I always took three threes for nine.

COST.   O Lord, sir, it were pity you should get your living by
  reckoning, sir.

BIRON.   How much is it?

COST.   O Lord, sir, the parties themselves, the actors, sir, will          530
  show whereuntil it doth amount: for mine own part, I am, as
  they say, but to parfect one man in one poor man, Pompion
  the Great, sir.

BIRON.   Art thou one of the Worthies?

502 *squier*] square, rule. He knows the length of his lady's foot, he knows how to humour
    her.
503 *laugh . . . eye*] laugh responsively to the slightest movement of her eye.
521 *beg us*] apply for the guardianship of us, as if we were imbeciles incapable of
    taking care of ourselves and our property.
532 *parfect*] The clown, absorbed by anxiety to be perfect in his part, uses the word
    "parfect," when he means to say "present," and mispronounces Pompey;
    "Pompion" is a word meaning pumpkin.

COST.  It pleased them to think me worthy of Pompion the
    Great: for mine own part, I know not the degree of the
    Worthy, but I am to stand for him.
BIRON.  Go, bid them prepare.
COST.  We will turn it finely off, sir; we will take some care.
                                                 *[Exit.*

KING.  Biron, they will shame us: let them not approach.          540
BIRON.  We are shame-proof, my lord: and 't is some policy
    To have one show worse than the king's and his company.
KING.  I say they shall not come.
PRIN.  Nay, my good lord, let me o'errule you now:
    That sport best pleases that doth least know how:
    Where zeal strives to content, and the contents
    Dies in the zeal of that which it presents:
    Their form confounded makes most form in mirth,
    When great things labouring perish in their birth.
BIRON.  A right description of our sport, my lord.          550

*Enter* ARMADO

ARM.  Anointed, I implore so much expense of thy royal sweet
    breath as will utter a brace of words.
      *[Converses apart with the* KING, *and delivers him a paper.*
PRIN.  Doth this man serve God?
BIRON.  Why ask you?
PRIN.  He speaks not like a man of God's making.
ARM.  That is all one, my fair, sweet, honey monarch; for, I
    protest, the schoolmaster is exceeding fantastical; too too
    vain, too too vain: but we will put it, as they say, to fortuna
    de la guerra. I wish you the peace of mind, most royal cou-
    plement!                           *[Exit.*          560
KING.  Here is like to be a good presence of Worthies. He pre-
    sents Hector of Troy; the swain, Pompey the Great; the
    parish curate, Alexander; Armado's page, Hercules; the
    pedant, Judas Maccabæus:
    And if these four Worthies in their first show thrive,
    These four will change habits, and present the other five.

544–549] The princess means that that sport pleases best where the actors are least skil-
    ful, and where their over-anxiety to please kills the true import of the perfor-
    mance, and has the unintended effect of provoking mirth. A more sympathetic
    sentiment is expressed by Theseus and Hippolyta in *Mids. N. Dr.*, V, i, 81–105,
    where Bottom and his incompetent allies, following the example of Holofernes
    and his friends, give a dramatic performance at court.
566] See note on V, i, 96, *supra*.

BIRON.    There is five in the first show.

KING.    You are deceived; 't is not so.

BIRON.    The pedant, the braggart, the hedge-priest, the fool and
the boy:—                                570
     Abate throw at novum, and the whole world again
     Cannot pick out five such, take each one in his vein.

KING.    The ship is under sail, and here she comes amain.

*Enter* COSTARD, *for Pompey*

COST.    I Pompey am,—

BOYET.                   You lie, you are not he.

COST.    I Pompey am,—

BOYET.                    With libbard's head on knee.

BIRON.    Well said, old mocker: I must needs be friends with
thee.

COST.    I Pompey am, Pompey surnamed the Big,—

DUM.    The Great.                                       580

COST.    It is, "Great," sir:—
                         Pompey surnamed the Great;
     That oft in field, with targe and shield, did make my foe to sweat:
     And travelling along this coast, I here am come by chance,
     And lay my arms before the legs of this sweet lass of France.
     If your ladyship would say, "Thanks, Pompey," I had done.

PRIN.    Great thanks, Great Pompey.

COST.    'T is not so much worth; but I hope I was perfect: I made
a little fault in "Great."

BIRON.    My hat to a halfpenny, Pompey proves the best Worthy.    590

*Enter* SIR NATHANIEL, *for Alexander*

NATH.    When in the world I lived, I was the world's commander;
     By east, west, north, and south, I spread my conquering might;
     My scutcheon plain declares that I am Alisander,—

BOYET.    Your nose says, no, you are not; for it stands too right.

BIRON.    Your nose smells "no" in this, most tender-smelling
knight.

PRIN.    The conqueror is dismay'd. Proceed, good Alexander.

NATH.    When in the world I lived, I was the world's commander,—

571 *Abate throw at novum*] "Novum," or more properly "Novem Quinque," was a game
     at dice, in which throws of nine or five were essential to victory. "Abate" here means
     "omit" or "bar." Biron says in effect, "bar a throw (of the *five*) at the game of novem
     quinque," and one will not find a more fortunate quintet.

594–595 *Your nose says, . . . knight*] Plutarch, in his life of Alexander, which
     Shakespeare read in North's translation, points out, like Biron, that the hero's head
     was fixed obliquely on his shoulders, and that his body exhaled a sweet savour.

BOYET.   Most true, 't is right; you were so, Alisander.
BIRON.   Pompey the Great,—
COST.   Your servant, and Costard.                                    600
BIRON.   Take away the conqueror, take away Alisander.
COST. [*To* SIR NATH]   O, sir, you have overthrown Alisander the
     conqueror! You will be scraped out of the painted cloth for
     this: your lion, that holds his poll-axe sitting on a close-stool,
     will be given to Ajax: he will be the ninth Worthy. A con-
     queror, and afeared to speak! run away for shame, Alisander.
     [NATH. *retires.*] There, an 't shall please you; a foolish mild
     man; an honest man, look you, and soon dashed. He is a
     marvellous good neighbour, faith, and a very good bowler:
     but, for Alisander,—alas, you see how 't is,—a little o'er-      610
     parted. But there are Worthies acoming will speak their
     mind in some other sort.
PRIN.   Stand aside, good Pompey.

*Enter* HOLOFERNES *for Judas; and* MOTH *for Hercules*

HOL.   Great Hercules is presented by this imp,
            Whose club kill'd Cerberus, that three-headed canis;
        And when he was a babe, a child, a shrimp,
            Thus did he strangle serpents in his manus.
        Quoniam he seemeth in minority,
        Ergo I come with this apology.

       Keep some state in thy exit, and vanish.          [MOTH *retires.*   620

            Judas I am,—

DUM.   A Judas!
HOL.   Not Iscariot, sir.

            Judas I am, ycliped Maccabæus.

DUM.   Judas Maccabæus clipt is plain Judas.
BIRON.   A kissing traitor. How art thou proved Judas?
HOL.   Judas I am,—
DUM.   The more shame for you, Judas.
HOL.   What mean you, sir?
BOYET.   To make Judas hang himself.                                  630
HOL.   Begin, sir; you are my elder.
BIRON.   Well followed: Judas was hanged on an elder.
HOL.   I will not be put out of countenance.
BIRON.   Because thou hast no face.

605 *Ajax*] a punning quibble on "a jakes."

HOL.   What is this?
BOYET.   A cittern-head.
DUM.   The head of a bodkin.
BIRON.   A Death's face in a ring.
LONG.   The face of an old Roman coin, scarce seen.
BOYET.   The pommel of Cæsar's falchion.                       640
DUM.   The carved-bone face on a flask.
BIRON.   Saint George's half-cheek in a brooch.
DUM.   Ay, and in a brooch of lead.
BIRON.   Ay, and worn in the cap of a tooth-drawer.
  And now forward; for we have put thee in countenance.
HOL.   You have put me out of countenance.
BIRON.   False: we have given thee faces.
HOL.   But you have out-faced them all.
BIRON.   An thou wert a lion, we would do so.
BOYET.   Therefore, as he is an ass, let him go.               650
  And so adieu, sweet Jude! nay, why dost thou stay?
DUM.   For the latter end of his name.
BIRON.   For the ass to the Jude; give it him:—Jud-as, away!
HOL.   This is not generous, not gentle, not humble.
BOYET.   A light for Monsieur Judas! it grows dark, he may
   stumble.                          [HOL. *retires.*
PRIN.   Alas, poor Maccabæus, how hath he been baited!

*Enter* ARMADO *for Hector*

BIRON.   Hide thy head, Achilles: here comes Hector in arms.
DUM.   Though my mocks come home by me, I will now be
   merry.
KING.   Hector was but a Troyan in respect of this.            660
BOYET.   But is this Hector?
KING.   I think Hector was not so clean-timbered.
LONG.   His leg is too big for Hector's.
DUM.   More calf, certain.
BOYET.   No; he is best indued in the small.
BIRON.   This cannot be Hector.
DUM.   He's a god or a painter; for he makes faces.
ARM.   The armipotent Mars, of lances the almighty,
   Gave Hector a gift,—
DUM.   A gilt nutmeg.                                          670
BIRON.   A lemon.
LONG.   Stuck with cloves.

636 *cittern-head*] the grotesquely carved head which often figured at the end of the key-
  board of a cithern or guitar.

DUM.   No, cloven.

ARM.   Peace!—

> The armipotent Mars, of lances the almighty,
>> Gave Hector a gift, the heir of Ilion;
> A man so breathed, that certain he would fight ye,
>> From morn till night, out of his pavilion.
> I am that flower,—

DUM.                   That mint.                   680

LONG.                  That columbine.

ARM.   Sweet Lord Longaville, rein thy tongue.

LONG.   I must rather give it the rein, for it runs against Hector.

DUM.   Ay, and Hector's a greyhound.

ARM.   The sweet war-man is dead and rotten; sweet chucks, beat
not the bones of the buried: when he breathed, he was a
man. But I will forward with my device. [*To the* PRINCESS]
Sweet royalty, bestow on me the sense of hearing.

PRIN.   Speak, brave Hector: we are much delighted.

ARM.   I do adore thy sweet Grace's slipper.                   690

BOYET. [*Aside to* DUM]   Loves her by the foot.

DUM. [*Aside to* BOYET]   He may not by the yard.

ARM.   This Hector far surmounted Hannibal,—

COST.   The party is gone, fellow Hector, she is gone; she is two
months on her way.

ARM.   What meanest thou?

COST.   Faith, unless you play the honest Troyan, the poor
wench is cast away: she's quick; the child brags in her belly
already: 't is yours.

ARM.   Dost thou infamonize me among potentates? thou shalt    700
die.

COST.   Then shall Hector be whipped for Jaquenetta that is
quick by him, and hanged for Pompey that is dead by him.

DUM.   Most rare Pompey!

BOYET.   Renowned Pompey!

BIRON.   Greater than great, great, great, great Pompey! Pompey
the Huge!

DUM.   Hector trembles.

BIRON.   Pompey is moved. More Ates, more Ates! stir them on!
stir them on!                                                  710

DUM.   Hector will challenge him.

BIRON.   Ay, if a' have no more man's blood in 's belly than will
sup a flea.

ARM.   By the north pole, I do challenge thee.

COST.   I will not fight with a pole, like a northern man: I'll slash;
I'll do it by the sword. I bepray you, let me borrow my arms
again.

DUM.   Room for the incensed Worthies!

COST.   I'll do it in my shirt.

DUM.   Most resolute Pompey!                      720

MOTH.   Master, let me take you a button-hole lower.
Do you not see Pompey is uncasing for the combat?
What mean you? You will lose your reputation.

ARM.   Gentlemen and soldiers, pardon me; I will not combat in
my shirt.

DUM.   You may not deny it: Pompey hath made the challenge.

ARM.   Sweet bloods, I both may and will.

BIRON.   What reason have you for 't?

ARM.   The naked truth of it is, I have no shirt; I go woolward for
penance.                                   730

BOYET.   True, and it was enjoined him in Rome for want of
linen: since when, I'll be sworn, he wore none but a dish-
clout of Jaquenetta's, and that a' wears next his heart for a
favour.

*Enter* MERCADE

MER.   God save you, Madam!

PRIN.   Welcome, Mercade;
But that thou interrupt'st our merriment.

MER.   I am sorry, madam; for the news I bring
Is heavy in my tongue. The king your father—

PRIN.   Dead, for my life!                        740

MER.   Even so; my tale is told.

BIRON.   Worthies, away! the scene begins to cloud.

ARM.   For mine own part, I breathe free breath. I have seen the
day of wrong through the little hole of discretion, and I will
right myself like a soldier.         [*Exeunt* WORTHIES.

KING.   How fares your majesty?

PRIN.   Boyet, prepare; I will away to-night.

KING.   Madam, not so; I do beseech you, stay.

715 *pole*] a quarterstaff, about six feet in length, and tipped with iron, in the difficult use
of which the Northern peasantry held a high reputation.

721 *take you a button-hole lower*] take you down a peg.

729 *woolward*] wearing only woollen instead of linen garments. Lodge in *Wits Miserie*,
1596 (Hunterian Club, p. 63), and Rowland's *Letting of Humours Blood*, 1600,
Satyre 5, both describe in like phrase a fashionable loafer, who, when "his shirt 's a
washing," "must *go woolward* for a time."

PRIN.　Prepare, I say. I thank you, gracious lords,
　　　For all your fair endeavours; and entreat,　　　　　750
　　　Out of a new-sad soul, that you vouchsafe
　　　In your rich wisdom to excuse, or hide,
　　　The liberal opposition of our spirits,
　　　If over-boldly we have borne ourselves
　　　In the converse of breath: your gentleness
　　　Was guilty of it. Farewell, worthy lord!
　　　A heavy heart bears not a nimble tongue:
　　　Excuse me so, coming too short of thanks
　　　For my great suit so easily obtain'd.
KING.　The extreme parts of time extremely forms　　　760
　　　All causes to the purpose of his speed;
　　　And often, at his very loose, decides
　　　That which long process could not arbitrate:
　　　And though the mourning brow of progeny
　　　Forbid the smiling courtesy of love
　　　The holy suit which fain it would convince;
　　　Yet, since love's argument was first on foot,
　　　Let not the cloud of sorrow justle it
　　　From what it purposed; since, to wail friends lost
　　　Is not by much so wholesome-profitable　　　　　770
　　　As to rejoice at friends but newly found.
PRIN.　I understand you not: my griefs are double.
BIRON.　Honest plain words best pierce the ear of grief;
　　　And by these badges understand the king.
　　　For your fair sakes have we neglected time,
　　　Play'd foul play with our oaths: your beauty, ladies,
　　　Hath much deform'd us, fashioning our humours
　　　Even to the opposed end of our intents:
　　　And what in us hath seem'd ridiculous,—
　　　As love is full of unbefitting strains;　　　　　780
　　　All wanton as a child, skipping, and vain;
　　　Form'd by the eye, and therefore, like the eye,

---

760–763 *The extreme . . . arbitrate*] The meaning seems to be, "When little time re-
　　mains, events fall out at the last minute, so as to make the available time quite suf-
　　ficient for the pending purpose, and at the very last moment things get finished off
　　with a readiness that the long and regular processes of business could not allow."
　　"At his very loose" means at the very moment of losing or parting, at the eleventh
　　hour; it may be a metaphor from the letting loose of the arrow in archery shooting.
772 *double*] This is the original reading. *Dull* is often substituted. The princess proba-
　　bly means that she has more griefs than her father's death to occupy her. She pos-
　　sibly regrets her recent frivolity while her father lay dying.

Full of strange shapes, of habits and of forms,
Varying in subjects as the eye doth roll
To every varied object in his glance:
Which parti-coated presence of loose love
Put on by us, if, in your heavenly eyes,
Have misbecomed our oaths and gravities,
Those heavenly eyes, that look into these faults,
Suggested us to make. Therefore, ladies,                        790
Our love being yours, the error that love makes
Is likewise yours: we to ourselves prove false,
By being once false for ever to be true
To those that make us both,—fair ladies, you:
And even that falsehood, in itself a sin,
Thus purifies itself, and turns to grace.

PRIN.   We have received your letters full of love;
    Your favours, the ambassadors of love;
    And, in our maiden council, rated them
    At courtship, pleasant jest and courtesy,                    800
    As bombast and as lining to the time:
    But more devout than this in our respects
    Have we not been; and therefore met your loves
    In their own fashion, like a merriment.

DUM.   Our letters, madam, show'd much more than jest.
LONG.   So did our looks.
ROS.                          We did not quote them so.
KING.   Now, at the latest minute of the hour,
    Grant us your loves.
PRIN.                          A time, methinks, too short       810
    To make a world-without-end bargain in.
    No, no, my lord, your grace is perjured much,
    Full of dear guiltiness; and therefore this:—
    If for my love, as there is no such cause,
    You will do aught, this shall you do for me:
    Your oath I will not trust; but go with speed
    To some forlorn and naked hermitage,
    Remote from all the pleasures of the world;
    There stay until the twelve celestial signs
    Have brought about the annual reckoning.                     820
    If this austere insociable life
    Change not your offer made in heat of blood;

783 *strange*] Capell's emendation for the original *straying*.
811 *world-without-end*] This epithet, doubtless derived from the liturgy, is used by
    Shakespeare once again—in *Sonnet* lvii, 5.

If frosts and fasts, hard lodging and thin weeds
Nip not the gaudy blossoms of your love,
But that it bear this trial, and last love;
Then, at the expiration of the year,
Come challenge me, challenge me by these deserts,
And, by this virgin palm now kissing thine,
I will be thine; and till that instant shut
My woeful self up in a mourning house,　　　　　830
Raining the tears of lamentation
For the remembrance of my father's death.
If this thou do deny, let our hands part,
Neither intitled in the other's heart.

KING.　If this, or more than this, I would deny,
　　To flatter up these powers of mine with rest,
　　The sudden hand of death close up mine eye!
　　Hence ever then my heart is in thy breast.

BIRON.　And what to me, my love? and what to me?

ROS.　You must be purged too, your sins are rack'd,　　840
　　You are attaint with faults and perjury:
　　Therefore if you my favour mean to get,
　　A twelvemonth shall you spend, and never rest,
　　But seek the weary beds of people sick.

DUM.　But what to me, my love? but what to me?
　　A wife?

KATH.　A beard, fair health, and honesty;
　　With three-fold love I wish you all these three.

DUM.　O, shall I say, I thank you, gentle wife?

KATH.　Not so, my lord; a twelvemonth and a day　　850
　　I'll mark no words that smooth-faced wooers say:
　　Come when the king doth to my lady come;
　　then, if I have much love, I'll give you some.

DUM.　I'll serve thee true and faithfully till then.

KATH.　Yet swear not, lest ye be forsworn again.

LONG.　What says Maria?

MAR.　　　　　　　At the twelvemonth's end
　　I'll change my black gown for a faithful friend.

LONG.　I'll stay with patience; but the time is long.

MAR.　The liker you; few taller are so young.　　860

839–844] These six lines, which Theobald put between brackets, were omitted by many subsequent editors. They present the first bald draft of lines 861–895, which Shakespeare alone intended to retain in the revised version of the piece. It is clear that they are redundant. Cf. *supra*, IV, iii, 302–303 and note.

BIRON.   Studies my lady? mistress, look on me;
   Behold the window of my heart, mine eye,
   What humble suit attends thy answer there:
   Impose some service on me for thy love.
ROS.   Oft have I heard of you, my Lord Biron,
   Before I saw you; and the world's large tongue
   Proclaims you for a man replete with mocks,
   Full of comparisons and wounding flouts,
   Which you on all estates will execute
   That lie within the mercy of your wit.                  870
   To weed this wormwood from your fruitful brain,
   And therewithal to win me, if you please,
   Without the which I am not to be won,
   You shall this twelvemonth term from day to day
   Visit the speechless sick, and still converse
   With groaning wretches; and your task shall be,
   With all the fierce endeavour of your wit
   To enforce the pained impotent to smile.
BIRON.   To move wild laughter in the throat of death?
   It cannot be; it is impossible:                        880
   Mirth cannot move a soul in agony.
ROS.   Why, that's the way to choke a gibing spirit,
   Whose influence is begot of that loose grace
   Which shallow laughing hearers give to fools:
   A jest's prosperity lies in the ear
   Of him that hears it, never in the tongue
   Of him that makes it: then, if sickly ears,
   Deaf'd with the clamours of their own dear groans,
   Will hear your idle scorns, continue then,
   And I will have you and that fault withal;              890
   But if they will not, throw away that spirit,
   And I shall find you empty of that fault,
   Right joyful of your reformation.
BIRON.   A twelvemonth! well; befall what will befall,
   I'll jest a twelvemonth in an hospital.
PRIN. [*To the* KING]   Ay, sweet my Lord; and so I take my leave.
KING.   No, madam; we will bring you on your way.
BIRON.   Our wooing doth not end like an old play;
   Jack hath not Jill: these ladies' courtesy
   Might well have made our sport a comedy.               900
KING.   Come, sir, it wants a twelvemonth and a day,
   And then 't will end.

BIRON.                    That's too long for a play.

*Re-enter* ARMADO

ARM.    Sweet Majesty, vouchsafe me, —
PRIN.    Was not that Hector?
DUM.    The worthy knight of Troy.
ARM.    I will kiss thy royal finger, and take leave. I am a votary; I
        have vowed to Jaquenetta to hold the plough for her sweet
        love three years. But, most esteemed greatness, will you hear
        the dialogue that the two learned men have compiled in      910
        praise of the owl and the cuckoo? it should have followed in
        the end of our show.
KING.    Call them forth quickly; we will do so.
ARM.    Holla! approach.

*Re-enter* HOLOFERNES, NATHANIEL, MOTH, COSTARD,
        *and others.*

        This side is Hiems, Winter, this Ver, the Spring; the one
        maintained by the owl, the other by the cuckoo. Ver, begin.

                        THE SONG

SPRING.            When daisies pied and violets blue
                      And lady-smocks all silver-white
                   And cuckoo-buds of yellow hue
                      Do paint the meadows with delight,         920
                   The cuckoo then, on every tree,
                   Mocks married men; for thus sings he,
                           Cuckoo;
                   Cuckoo, cuckoo: O word of fear,
                   Unpleasing to a married ear!

                   When shepherds pipe on oaten straws,
                      And merry larks are ploughmen's clocks,
                   When turtles tread, and rooks, and daws,
                      And maidens bleach their summer smocks,
                   The cuckoo then, on every tree,              930
                   Mocks married men; for thus sings he,
                           Cuckoo;
                   Cuckoo, cuckoo: O word of fear,
                   Unpleasing to a married ear!

WINTER.            When icicles hang by the wall,
                      And Dick the shepherd blows his nail,
                   And Tom bears logs into the hall.
                      And milk comes frozen home in pail,

When blood is nipp'd and ways be foul,
Then nightly sings the staring owl,           940
       Tu-whit;
Tu-who, a merry note,
While greasy Joan doth keel the pot.

When all aloud the wind doth blow,
    And coughing drowns the parson's saw,
And birds sit brooding in the snow,
    And Marion's nose looks red and raw,
When roasted crabs hiss in the bowl,
Then nightly sings the staring owl,
       Tu-whit;           950
Tu-who, a merry note,
While greasy Joan doth keel the pot.

ARM.    The words of Mercury are harsh after the songs of Apollo.
    You that way,—we this way.            [*Exeunt.*

---

948 *roasted crabs*] roasted crab apples.
952 *keel*] Cf. Marston's *What you will* (1607): "Faith, Dorsicus, my brain boils. *Keel* it,
    *keel* it, or all the fat's in the fire," *i.e.* stir, skim, or pour in something cold in order
    to prevent the pot from boiling over.